Downtown 2

English for Work and Life

Workbook

JOHN CHAPMAN

THOMSON

HEINLE

Australia • Canada • Mexico • Singapore • Spain • United Kingdom • United States

Downtown 2
English for Work and Life
Workbook
John Chapman

Publisher, Adult and Academic: James W. Brown
Senior Acquisitions Editor, Adult and Academic: Sherrise Roehr
Director of Product Development: Anita Raducanu
Development Editor: Kasia McNabb
Development Editor: Sarah Barnicle
Development Editor: Rebecca Tarver Chase
Director of Product Marketing: Amy Mabley
Senior Field Marketing Manager: Donna Lee Kennedy
Product Marketing Manager: Laura Needham
Editorial Assistant: Katherine Reilly

Senior Production Editor: Maryellen E. Killeen
Senior Print Buyer: Mary Beth Hennebury
Design and Composition: Parkwood Composition
Project Management: Tünde Dewey
Cover Design: Lori Stuart
Cover Art: Jean-François Allaux
Printer: P. A. Hutchison

Printed in the United States of America
1 2 3 4 5 6 7 8 9 10   09 08 07 06

For more information contact Thomson Heinle, 25 Thomson Place, Boston, MA 02210 USA, or visit our Internet site at elt.thomson.com

For permission to use material from this text or product, submit a request online at http://www.thomsonrights.com

Any additional questions about permissions can be submitted by email to thomsonrights@thomson.com

ISBN: 0-8384-5163-2

Contents

Personal Information

Chapter 1

Vocabulary

1 **Complete the lists with words from the box. Use each word once.**

| eraser ~~gray~~ uncle blond work schedule ~~chalkboard~~ curly aunt |
| dark supervisor ~~mother~~ chalk cousins ~~job~~ pencil sharpener coworkers |

1. Hair

   gray _____

   _____

   _____

   _____

2. Classroom

   chalkboard _____

   _____

   _____

   _____

3. Family

   mother _____

   _____

   _____

   _____

4. Office

   job _____

   _____

   _____

   _____

2 **Complete the sentences with words from the box.**

| country | nationality | coworker | bald | ~~hobby~~ |

1. Q: What is your _____ _hobby_ _____ ?

   A: I like to dance.

2. Q: What is your _____ ?

   A: I'm Chinese.

3. Q: Is Maria your classmate?

   A: No, she's my _____ .

4. Q: Does he have long hair?

   A: No, he's _____ .

5. Q: What _____ are you from?

   A: I'm from Mexico.

My Name is Jessica

1 Complete the conversation.

1. **Jessica:** Hello. ___d___
2. **Lin:** Hi, Jessica. _____
3. **Jessica:** I'm from Colombia. _____
4. **Lin:** _____ What do you do?
5. **Jessica:** _____
6. **Lin:** _____
7. **Jessica:** _____

a. How long were you an artist?
b. I am Lin Lee.
c. I'm from Vietnam.
d. ~~My name is Jessica.~~
e. For three years.
f. I'm a student now. I was an artist in my country.
g. Where are you from?

2 Fill in your student registration form.

STUDENT REGISTRATION FORM
FOR NEW AND RETURNING STUDENTS

LAST NAME: _____

FIRST NAME: _____

DATE: _____

ADDRESS: _____

CITY: _____

STATE: _____ ZIP CODE: _____

TELEPHONE: (_____) _____

DATE OF BIRTH: _____

PLACE OF BIRTH: _____

3 Circle the correct word.

1. **Was /** (**Were**) **you** a teacher in your country?

2. We **wasn't / weren't** students.

3. **Was / Were** they lawyers?

4. Lin **was / were** an artist.

5. She **wasn't / weren't** an accountant.

4 Write sentences in the past tense. Use the words below and *was, wasn't, were,* or *weren't*.

1. (Dina / not a student)

   Dina wasn't a student.

2. (She / a soccer player)

   _____

3. (We / not teammates)

   _____

4. (She / born in 1982)

   _____

5. (I / born in 1980)

   _____

5 Write questions. Use the words below and *was* or *were*.

1. (Lin / a lawyer?)

   Was Lin a lawyer?

2. (you / a student?)

   _____

3. (your classmates / from Mexico?)

   _____

4. (your mother / a teacher?)

   _____

5. (Oscar / a soccer player?)

   _____

Meet My Family

1 **Complete the conversation. Use the phrases in the box. You will use some phrases more than once.**

~~Let me introduce~~	These are my	His name is	Hello
Her name is	Their names are	Nice to meet	This is my

A: _Let me introduce_ you to my family. _____ sister. _____ Sue.

B: _____, Sue.

A: _____ brother. _____ Andy.

B: _____ you, Sue and Andy.

A: _____ parents. _____ Helen and Sam.

B: _____, Helen. _____, Sam.

_____ you.

2 **Complete the sentences with words from the box. Use each word once.**

thin	mustache	long	blond	straight	tall

1. He's not short. He's _____tall_____ .

2. He has long, _____ hair.

3. He has a _____ .

4. She's not heavy. She's _____ .

5. She has _____, black hair.

6. Her hair isn't curly. It's _____ .

3 Write questions and statements. Put the words in order.

1. (short / tall / she / or / is)

   Is she short or tall?

2. (tall / Henry / is / how)

   _____

3. (ten / five / he's / foot)

   _____

4. (he / thin / heavy / is / or)

   _____

5. (he / much / weigh / does / how)

   _____

4 Maria is introducing her family. Complete the sentences. Use the words in the box.

brother	brother-in-law	nephew	~~sister~~	mother	niece

Roberto, Lupe, Martin, Dulce

1. This is a picture of my family. This is my _____*sister*_____ Lupe.

2. This is my _____ Roberto.

3. That's my _____ Martin.

4. And that's my _____ Dulce.

5. Martin and Dulce are _____ and sister.

6. My mother is also Lupe's _____ .

5 **Complete the sentences with the correct object pronoun from the box.**

me	him	~~her~~	it	us	them

1. She is my supervisor. I work for ___*her.*___

2. It was my birthday. People gave gifts to _____ .

3. That's my dictionary. Please give _____ to me.

4. His mother and father are in Texas. He called _____ on the telephone.

5. Mother cooked dinner for you and me. She made pizza for _____ .

6. That's Frank's book. Give it to _____ .

6 **Complete the questions and answers under each picture.**

1. Q: *Does she have* _____ long hair?

   A: *Yes, she does.* _____

2. Q: _____ thin?

   A: _____

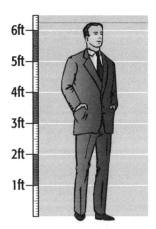

3. Q: _____ wavy hair?

   A: _____

4. Q: _____ tall?

   A: _____

First Day at Work

① Complete the sentences. Use the words in the box.

Who	What	Where	When	Why

1. ___*What*___ is your name?

2. _____ do you finish work?

3. _____ are you talking to?

4. _____ do you live with your parents?

5. _____ is the meeting—in Room 12 or Room 14?

6. _____ is your job title?

7. _____ is your supervisor?

8. _____ is her office?

9. _____ do you leave on vacation?

10. _____ do you like her?

② Complete the conversation. Use the words in the box.

sure	maybe	the cafeteria	~~on the job~~	questions	anything

A: This is my first day _____ *on the job.* _____

B: Is there _____ I can help you with? Do you have
   any _____ ?

A: _____ just one.

B: OK, _____ .

A: Where is _____ ?

3 **Study Jim's schedule for today. Read the answers. Complete the questions using When, Where, What, and Who.**

Jim's Schedule		
Time	**Place**	
9:00	Room 111	go to English class
10:00	Room 102	meet Mr. Ryan
11:00	Library	study with Amy
12:00	Cafeteria	eat lunch with Ali

1. Q: _What does he_ _____ do in Room 111 at 9:00?

   A: He goes to English class.

2. Q: _____ meet Mr. Ryan at 10:00?

   A: In Room 102.

3. Q: _____ go to the library?

   A: He goes to the library at 11:00.

4. Q: _____ eat lunch?

   A: In the cafeteria.

5. Q: _____ eat lunch with?

   A: He eats lunch with Ali.

4 **Complete the sentences.**

1. I like to watch __e__ .   a. museums

2. They play _____ .   b. soccer

3. We go _____ .   c. pictures

4. She goes to _____ .   d. hiking

5. He likes to _____ .   e. ~~television~~

6. I paint _____ .   f. dance

1 Bubble the correct answers.

	a	b	c

1. My husband's sister is my _____ .
   a) aunt   b) cousin   c) sister-in-law   ○ ○ ○

2. Where do you work?
   a) At 10:00.   b) In an office.   c) I'm a lawyer.   ○ ○ ○

3. Q: _____ ?   A: In 1980.
   a) When were you born?   b) Where are you from?   c) What do you do?   ○ ○ ○

4. Q: _____ ?   A: I'm an accountant.
   a) How are you?   b) Who do you live with?   c) What do you do?   ○ ○ ○

5. What is your hobby?
   a) I ski.   b) I'm Vietnamese.   c) I have long, straight hair. ○ ○ ○

2 Read Allen's story. Answer the questions. Use complete sentences.

Allen's New Life

Allen is 30 years old and new in town. He lives in New York City now. He is a computer programmer. He lives with two coworkers and another friend.

Allen studied math and computer programming in college. He came to New York for his first job. He works for a large bank. The pay is not very good, but he likes the work. He is also going to school at night. He wants to learn more and get a better job.

Allen's family lives in Boston. He sometimes visits them on weekends. Allen has several hobbies. He plays tennis and he runs in the park. He also likes to watch soccer games on TV.

1. How old is Allen? _He's 30 years old._____

2. Where does he live now? _____

3. What is his job? _____

4. What did he study in college? _____

5. Who does he work for? _____

6. What does he do at night? _____

7. Where does his family live? _____

8. What does he play? _____

Daily Activities

Chapter 2

Vocabulary

1 **Complete the sentences.**

1. He's delivering __c__ .
2. He's cutting ____ .
3. She's doing ____ .
4. He's making ____ .
5. They're paying ____ .
6. I'm watering ____ .
7. He's cashing ____ .
8. We're cooking ____ .

a. the bed
b. hair
c. ~~mail~~
d. the garden
e. laundry
f. bills
g. dinner
h. a check

2 **Circle the item that doesn't belong.**

1. priority mail	(laundry)	letters
2. personal trainer	customer	salesperson
3. hairstylist	shopping	hair salon
4. cutting hair	café	coffee
5. clothing store	restaurant	school
6. office	package	mail carrier
7. housework	homework	making beds
8. drugstore	prescription	exercise
9. bank	priority mail	check
10. groceries	letters	supermarket

What's She Doing?

1 **Complete the questions and answers under each picture.**

1. Q: How often _does she wash the windows_ ?

   A: _She washes the windows_ twice a month.

2. Q: How often _____ ?

   A: _____ once a week.

3. Q: How often _____ ?

   A: _____ every night.

4. Q: How often _____ ?

   A: _____ every day.

5. Q: How often _____ ?

   A: _____ once a week.

6. Q: How often _____ ?

   A: _____ twice a week.

2 **Complete the sentences with the correct form of *make* or *do*.**

1. Do you usually ___do___ the dishes?

2. How often does Linda _____ a cake?

3. Larry _____ his bed once a week.

4. Do you always _____ your homework?

5. How often do you _____ phone calls to your country?

6. My brother _____ the shopping on Saturday mornings.

7. Do you ever _____ the housework?

8. They _____ breakfast at 7:00.

9. Do you _____ your exercises every day?

10. My sister _____ the laundry every Friday.

3 **Match the numbers with the words.**

1. 100% of the time __e__   a. seldom

2. 90% of the time _____   b. rarely

3. 60% of the time _____   c. usually

4. 50% of the time _____   d. sometimes

5. 20% of the time _____   e. ~~always~~

6. 10% of the time _____   f. never

7. 0% of the time _____   g. often

4 **Complete these sentences about yourself. Use an adverb of frequency.**

1. I _____ do the laundry.

2. I _____ make repairs at home.

3. I _____ eat a big breakfast.

4. I am _____ asleep by 12:00.

5. I _____ dance.

5 Write statements with frequency words. Put the words in order.

1. (always / make / bed / I / my own)
   I always make my own bed.

2. (cleans / seldom / the bathroom / she)
   _____

3. (late / rarely / for class / arrive / we)
   _____

4. (does / on Monday / usually / he / the grocery shopping)
   _____

5. (sometimes / late / I / for work / arrive)
   _____

6. (makes / never / my father / dinner)
   _____

7. (asleep / sometimes / by 9:00 / is / she)
   _____

8. (my children / often / with their homework / help / I)
   _____

6 Complete the conversations. Use the correct verb tense.

1. Q: What is Jessica doing?

   A: _She's calling her mother._ (call her mother)

   Q: How often _does she call her mother?_

   A: _She calls her mother_ once a week.

2. Q: What are they doing?

   A: _____ (do the laundry)

   Q: How often _____ ?

   A: _____ twice a month.

3. Q: What are you doing?

   A: _____ (paying bills)

   Q: How often _____ ?

   A: _____ every week.

4. Q: What is Luis doing?

   A: _____ (cleaning his room)

   Q: How often _____ ?

   A: _____ once a year.

Jessica's Neighborhood

1 **Look at the map. Answer the questions.**

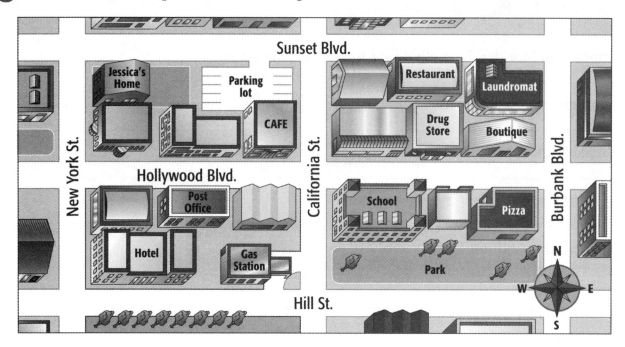

1. Is Hill Street on the north or south side of the city?

   Hill Street is on the south side of the city.

2. Is the school on Hollywood Boulevard?

   _____

3. Is there a parking lot on Burbank Boulevard?

   _____

4. What is on the northeast corner of Hill Street and California Street?

   _____

5. What street is on the north side of the city?

   _____

6. What is on the southwest corner of Burbank and Sunset?

   _____

7. Is there a hotel on Hill Street?

   _____

8. What directions does New York Street run?

   _____

❷ Complete the conversations.

1. Q: Where is John?

   A: _He's at the office._____ (the office)

   Q: What's he doing there?

   A: I'm not sure. _He could be writing letters._____ (write letters)

2. Q: Where is Tony?

   A: _____ (the bedroom)

   Q: What's he doing in there?

   A: I'm not sure. _____ (make the bed)

3. Q: Where are your mother and father?

   A: _____ (the kitchen)

   Q: What are they doing in there?

   A: I'm not sure. _____ (make coffee)

4. Q: Where is your daughter?

   A: _____ (the grocery store)

   Q: What is she doing there?

   A: I'm not sure. _____ (buying ice cream)

❸ Read the questions. Circle the correct words in the answers.

1. Q: Where is Anna?

   A: I'm not sure. She **(is probably)** / **could be** at school.   (90 % sure)

2. Q: Where is Jessica?

   A: I'm not sure. She **is probably** / **could be** at the hair salon.   (10% sure)

3. Q: Where is Robert?

   A: I'm not sure. He **is probably** / **could be** at home.   (25% sure)

4. Q: Where is the teacher?

   A: I'm not sure. He **is probably** / **could be** in the cafeteria.   (80% sure)

5. Q: Where is your brother?

   A: I'm not sure. He **is probably** / **could be** at Tina's house.   (30% sure)

6. Q: Where are the other students?

   A: I'm not sure. They **are probably** / **could be** in the library.   (10% sure)

What Do You Do at Work?

1 Use the postal rate chart to complete the conversations below.

POSTAL RATE CHART			
FIRST CLASS MAIL	**PRIORITY MAIL**	**BOOK RATE**	**EXPRESS MAIL**
Up to 1 oz. = $.39 2 oz. = $.63 3 oz. = $.87 4 oz. = $1.11	Up to 1 lb. = $4.05 2 lb. = $4.20 3 lb. = $5.00 4 lb. = $5.60	Up to 1 lb. = $1.59 2 lb. = $2.07 3 lb. = $2.55 4 lb. = $3.03	Up to 8 oz. = $14.40 2 lb. = $18.80 3 lb. = $22.20 4 lb. = $25.50

1. Q: I'd like to send this by express mail. How much does it cost?

   A: Let's see. How much does it weigh?

   Q: It weighs 8 ounces.

   A: Then it costs _$14.40._____

2. Q: I'd like to send this by book rate. How much does it cost?

   A: Let's see. How much does it weigh?

   Q: It weighs 4 pounds.

   A: Then it costs _____ .

3. Q: I'd like to send this by priority mail. How much does it cost?

   A: Let's see. How much does it weigh?

   Q: It weighs 3 pounds.

   A: Then it costs _____ .

4. Q: I'd like to send this by first-class mail. How much does it cost?

   A: Let's see. How much does it weigh?

   Q: It weighs 3 ounces.

   A: Then it costs _____ .

5. Q: I'd like to send this by book rate. How much does it cost?

   A: Let's see. How much does it weigh?

   Q: It weighs 1 pound.

   A: Then it costs _____ .

6. Q: I'd like to send this by first-class mail. How much does it cost?

   A: Let's see. How much does it weigh?

   Q: It weighs 1 ounce.

   A: Then it costs _____ .

❷ Complete each sentence with the correct form of the verb.

1. I ___see___ (see) your book. It's on the table.
2. I _____ (study) right now.
3. I always _____ (study) at night.
4. That computer _____ (cost) a lot!
5. We _____ (believe) you.
6. You _____ (know) all the answers on the test.
7. I _____ (listen) to the radio right now.
8. I _____ (listen) to the radio every day.
9. She _____ (understand) the lesson very well today.
10. I _____ (like) this pizza a lot.

❸ Match the sentence halves.

1. A mail carrier __e__ .
2. A hairstylist _____ .
3. A computer animator _____ .
4. A student _____ .
5. A personal trainer _____ .
6. A salesperson _____ .
7. A bank employee _____ .

a. prepares for tests
b. works in a store
c. cuts hair
d. works in a health club
e. ~~delivers letters~~
f. cashes checks
g. uses software programs

Review

1 Bubble the correct answers.

	a b

1. What is she doing?
   a) She's making the dishes.   b) She's doing the dishes.   ○   ○
2. What is her name?
   a) I am not knowing it.   b) I don't know.   ○   ○
3. Is Jessica at the gym?
   a) Yes, she is doing exercises.   b) Yes, she is making exercises.   ○   ○
4. What are they doing?
   a) They're making dinner.   b) They're doing dinner.   ○   ○
5. Is that a good book?
   a) Yes, I am liking it a lot.   b) Yes, I like it a lot.   ○   ○

2 Read Raquel's story. Circle *True* or *False*.

Raquel and Her Friends

Raquel is 25 years old. She lives in Miami, Florida. She works and goes to school, and she also does housework. In her home country, she just went to school. Her father worked and gave her money. Her mother did the housework. Now she makes her own meals and pays her own bills, but she doesn't do the laundry. Her roommate, Sarah, does it, and Raquel cooks dinner for Sarah.

Raquel likes her neighborhood very much. The people are all very friendly. Her roommate, Sarah, works in a nearby café. She walks to work. There is also a health club in the neighborhood. Raquel and Sarah often exercise together in the evening.

Raquel's friend Marco lives near her. Marco works for the post office. He is a mail clerk. The post office is downtown. It takes him over an hour to get there, but he likes his job a lot. On weekends, Marco and Raquel sometimes ride their bikes to the post office —just for fun.

1. Raquel is 30 years old.	True	False
2. Raquel's father gives her money now.	True	False
3. Raquel does her own laundry.	True	False
4. Raquel's neighbors are friendly.	True	False
5. Sarah works in a health club.	True	False
6. Marco is a mail clerk.	True	False
7. The post office is near the health club.	True	False
8. Raquel and Marco ride their bikes every day.	True	False

 **Food**

Vocabulary

❶ Complete the lists with words from the box. Use each word once.

soda	cabinet	dishes	~~kitchen table~~
~~milk~~	~~corn~~	turkey	refrigerator
sweet potatoes	counter	~~glasses~~	bowls
coffee	stuffing	tea	plates

1. Thanksgiving foods

   _corn_____

   _____

   _____

   _____

2. Parts of a kitchen

   _kitchen table_____

   _____

   _____

   _____

3. Drinks

   _milk_____

   _____

   _____

   _____

4. Things you put food on or in

   _glasses_____

   _____

   _____

   _____

❷ Complete the sentences with words from the box. Use each word once.

butter	napkin	~~cookies~~	freezer	silverware	ice	bread	~~ice cream~~

1. You can serve _____ice cream_____ and _____cookies_____ for dessert.

2. You put a _____ and _____ next to each plate.

3. You put _____ on _____ .

4. You make _____ in the _____ .

Thanksgiving Dinner

❶ Circle the correct answer.

1. cheese	a. count	**b. noncount**		7. bread	a. count	b. noncount
2. corn	a. count	b. noncount		8. napkin	a. count	b. noncount
3. butter	a. count	b. noncount		9. ice	a. count	b. noncount
4. stuffing	a. count	b. noncount		10. milk	a. count	b. noncount
5. plate	a. count	b. noncount		11. cookie	a. count	b. noncount
6. candle	a. count	b. noncount		12. coffee	a. count	b. noncount

❷ Write questions. Put the words in order.

1. (ice cream / is / in the refrigerator / any / there)

   Is there any ice cream in the refrigerator?

2. (cookies / on the plate / any / there / are)

   _____

3. (there / silverware / any / is / on the table)

   _____

4. (are / napkins / in the cabinet / there / any)

   _____

5. (is / salad / in the bowl / there / any)

   _____

6. (carrots / any / in the salad / there / are)

   _____

❸ Circle the correct word in each question and answer.

1. Q: How **much** / **many** cookies would you like? A: Just **a little** / **a few.**
2. Q: How **much** / **many** milk do you want? A: Just **a little** / **a few.**
3. Q: How **much** / **many** ice cream is in the freezer? A: Just **a little** / **a few.**
4. Q: How **much** / **many** napkins do we need? A: Just **a little** / **a few.**
5. Q: How **much** / **many** cake do you want? A: Just **a little** / **a few.**

4 Complete the sentences with words from the box. Use each word once.

| can   tub   ~~plate~~   bottle   container   box |

1. It's a __plate__ of cookies.   2. It's a _____ of rice.   3. It's a _____ of butter.

4. It's a _____ of ketchup.   5. It's a _____ of milk.   6. It's a _____ of soup.

5 Circle the correct word in each question and answer.

1. There isn't **some / (any)** stuffing in the turkey.

2. Would you like **some / any** tea?

3. There are **some / any** dishes on the counter.

4. She doesn't want **some / any** ice cream right now.

5. There is **some / any** milk in the container.

6. There aren't **some / any** bowls in the cupboard.

6 Answer the questions about yourself.

EXAMPLES: How much rice do you eat?   _A lot._ OR _Not much._ OR _____ A little. _____

How many pancakes can you eat?   _A lot._ OR _____ Just a few. _____

1. How much soda do you drink? _____

2. How much coffee do you drink? _____

3. How much ice cream is in your freezer at home? _____

4. How many bananas do you eat each week? _____

5. How many meals do you have every day? _____

6. How many cookies do you usually eat? _____

What Do We Need?

❶ Bubble the correct answers.

	a	b	c	d

1. Are there _____ plates on the table?
   a) a   b) an   c) some   d) any   ○   ○   ○   ○
2. There is _____ glass next to the plate.
   a) a   b) an   c) some   d) any   ○   ○   ○   ○
3. There aren't _____ chips in the bowl.
   a) a   b) an   c) some   d) any   ○   ○   ○   ○
4. Is there _____ apple in the refrigerator?
   a) a   b) an   c) some   d) any   ○   ○   ○   ○
5. There is _____ milk in the glass.
   a) a   b) an   c) some   d) any   ○   ○   ○   ○
6. I need _____ plate for the cookies.
   a) a   b) an   c) some   d) any   ○   ○   ○   ○
7. There aren't _____ glasses in the cupboard.
   a) a   b) an   c) some   d) any   ○   ○   ○   ○
8. There is _____ onion on the counter.
   a) a   b) an   c) some   d) any   ○   ○   ○   ○
9. Can I have _____ turkey please?
   a) a   b) an   c) some   d) any   ○   ○   ○   ○
10. There isn't _____ bread on the table.
    a) a   b) an   c) some   d) any   ○   ○   ○   ○

❷ Complete the conversations about the future. Use *be* + *going to.*

1. Q: _Is he going to go shopping?_____   (he / go shopping)

   A: Yes, _he is._____

2. Q: _____   (they / stay home)

   A: No, _____.

3. Q: _____   (you / buy turkey)

   A: No, _____.

4. Q: _____   (she / cook dinner)

   A: Yes, _____.

5. Q: _____   (we / make bread)

   A: No, _____.

6. Q: _____   (he / eat dessert)

   A: Yes, _____.

③ Complete the sentences with a present tense verb + infinitive.

1. José _____*likes to play*_____ soccer on Saturdays. (like / play)

2. Anna _____ dinner at a restaurant tonight. (want / have)

3. She _____ to the movies tonight. (not want / go)

4. John _____ television. (love / watch)

5. I _____ (not like / do) the dishes.

6. They _____ (not want / clean) their rooms.

7. We _____ late. (love / sleep)

8. You _____ cake. (like / eat)

④ Answer the questions about the foods.

NUTRITION FACTS — BENNY'S BEAN SOUP
Ingredients: water, great northern beans, enriched macaroni, egg whites, celery, tomato paste, soybean oil, salt, Romano cheese, garlic powder
Nutrition facts:
Total fat: 3.5 g
Saturated fat: 1 g
Trans fat: 0g
Cholesterol: 0 mg
Sodium: 890 mg
Carbohydrate: 25 g
Protein: 7 g

NUTRITION FACTS — VEGGIE BURGER
Ingredients: water, soy protein, corn protein, onion powder, sugar, wheat flour, salt
Nutrition facts:
Total fat: 6 g
Saturated fat: 1 g
Trans fat: 0 g
Cholesterol: 0 g
Sodium: 430 mg
Carbohydrate: 15 g
Protein: 11 g

1. Which ingredient is found in the largest amount? _*water*_____

2. Does the soup have more macaroni or beans? _____

3. Which ingredient is found in the smallest amount? _____

4. Is there more celery or tomato paste? _____

5. How much fat does the soup have? _____

6. How much protein does it have? _____

7. Which ingredient is found in the largest amount? _____

8. Does the burger have more onion powder or sugar? _____

9. Which ingredient is found in the smallest amount? _____

10. How much saturated fat does the burger have? _____

11. How much sodium is in the burger? _____

12. How much protein does it have? _____

❺ Complete the conversations using information from the coupons. Use *a, an, some,* or *any.*

> **Save at the Dairy Place!**
> Dairy Fresh Milk — Half Gallon
> Usually: $3.99 — This weekend only $2.99

> **Special on Thanksgiving Turkeys!**
> **Save 50%!**
> Usually $2.00 a pound.
> This weekend only $1.00 a pound.

1. Q: What are you going to buy?

   A: *I'm going to buy some milk.*

   Q: How much is it?

   A: The regular price is *$3.99*   but this weekend it's only *$2.99.*

2. Q: What are you going to buy?

   A: _____

   Q: How much is it?

   A: It's _____ off. It's _____ a pound.

> **Special Super Duper Savings!**
> **Moo Cow Ice Cream — 25% off**
> Usually: $4.00 a gallon.
> This Friday only $3.00.

> **Holiday Candles — 50% Off!**
> Save $3.00 on a box of 12 candles

3. Q: What are you going to buy?

   A: _____

   Q: How much is it?

   A: It's _____ off. It's only _____ .

4. Q: What are you going to buy?

   A: _____

   Q: How much are they?

   A: They're usually _____ a box. But now they're only _____ a box.

> **Special On Carrots!**
> Regular price: $2.00 a bag
> Today only: $1.00 a bag

> **Save $1.00 on Piney Paper Napkins**
> Regular Price: $1.99
> Today only: $.99

5. Q: Are you going to buy _____ vegetables?

   A: Yes, I'm going to get _____ carrots.

   Q: How much are they?

   A: They're 50% _____ — only $1.00 a bag.

6. Q: What are you going to buy?

   A: _____

   Q: How much are they?

   A: They're _____ off — only $.99 a package.

What Would You Like?

① Circle the correct words in each sentence.

1. **(Would you like)** / **Do you like** to go to the movies tonight?

2. **She likes** / **She would like** summer because it's so warm.

3. **Would he like** / **Does he like** to be a teacher when he is older?

4. **He wouldn't like** / **He doesn't like** his middle name.

5. **Would she love** / **Does she love** her parents?

6. **Would you like** / **Do you like** to have a million dollars?

7. **Tom likes** / **Tom would like** to live to be 100 years old.

8. **They like** / **They would like** to meet the president of the United States.

9. **How would you like** / **How do you like** your new car?

10. **Do you like** / **Would you like** to marry me?

② Complete the conversations. Use the words *would, do, does, don't, doesn't, like,* and *likes.*

1. Q: ___Would___ you _____like_____ coffee with breakfast this morning?
   A: No, but I _would like_ some tea, thanks.

2. Q: _____ you _____ the shirt I'm wearing today?
   A: Yes, and I _____ your shoes, too.

3. Q: Linda moved to Florida. _____ she _____ it?
   A: Yes, she _____ the sunny weather.

4. Q: _____ your parents _____ to visit you?
   A: Yes, they _____ to visit me, but they don't have time this year.

5. Q: _____ you _____ to visit Africa someday?
   A: Yes, I _____ to see the elephants.

6. Q: _____ you _____ your new apartment?
   A: No, I _____ the noisy halls.

7. Q: _____ your sister _____ to go to college?
   A: Yes, she _____, but she doesn't have enough money.

8. Q: _____ you like some milk to go with those cookies?
   A: Yes, I _____.

9. Q: _____ the class usually finish at 10:00?
   A: Yes, it _____ .

10. Q: _____ the teacher _____ to have a two-hour class?
    A: Yes, she _____, but another class uses the room at 10:00.

3 **Complete each sentence with an infinitive (to + verb) or a gerund (verb + -ing). If both the infinitive and gerund are correct, write both forms of the verb.**

1. I would like _____*to go*_____ to the movies tonight. (go)

2. She likes _____ . (swim)

3. I like _____ TV. (watch)

4. Would you like _____ my car? (use)

5. They like _____ in France. (live)

6. She would like _____ married. (get)

7. He doesn't like _____ homework every night. (do)

8. Would he like _____ a flat screen TV? (buy)

9. They wouldn't like _____ dinner. (cook)

10. We like _____ up late. (stay)

4 **Fix the mistakes in the incorrect sentences. If the sentence is correct, write *correct.***

1. I like drive my friend's car.

   *I like to drive my friend's car.*_____ OR *I like driving my friend's car.*_____

2. They would likes to visit Brazil. _____

3. She like to buy a new car. _____

4. I would like going home now, please. _____

5. They would like give you one of their puppies. _____

6. I like exercising very much. _____

7. Do you like to exercise? _____

8. I would like having a party next weekend. _____

9. She like getting up early in the morning. _____

10. She would likes to have another child. _____

11. He like to ride his bicycle every day. _____

12. They like studying in the library. _____

Review

① Bubble the correct answers.

a   b   c

1. People usually keep _____ in the refrigerator.
   a) candles   b) butter   c) silverware   ○ ○ ○
2. The napkins are on the _____ .
   a) counter   b) kitchen   c) garlic   ○ ○ ○
3. How _____ pudding would you like?
   a) many   b) some   c) much   ○ ○ ○
4. This week toasters are 25% _____.
   a) price   b) off   c) cost   ○ ○ ○
5. Can I have _____ coffee?
   a) some   b) any   c) much   ○ ○ ○

② Read Brenda's story. Answer the questions. Use complete sentences.

Trying New Foods

Brenda works as a waitress at the Downtown International Restaurant. Her friends come there to eat, and she likes serving them new kinds of food. Her friend Kumi is from Japan. Last week Kumi tried drinking cappuccino for the first time. She thought it looked strange, but she liked it a lot.

Brenda's friend Patel is from India. He usually eats Indian food, so Brenda said he should try something really different. She gave him a plate of lasagna, but he didn't like it very much. Patel said he would like to try eating raw fish, so Brenda served him some sushi. When he finished it, he said he wasn't going to order that dish again. Brenda likes serving her friends new foods.

1. Where does Brenda work? _She works at the Downtown International Restaurant._
2. Where is Kumi from? _____
3. Where is Patel from? _____
4. What did Kumi try drinking? _____
5. Did she like it? _____
6. What didn't Patel like? _____
7. What did he want to eat? _____
8. Is he going to order it again? _____

Housing

Vocabulary

1 **Complete the lists with words from the box. Use each word once.**

~~garage~~	~~fireplace~~	lamp	coffee table
sofa	window	mini blinds	night table
dresser	yard	~~bedspread~~	end table
~~skylight~~	garden	grill	alarm clock

1. Things outside the house

   garage _____

   _____

   _____

2. Things in the bedroom

   bedspread _____

   _____

   _____

3. Things in the living room

   fireplace _____

   _____

   _____

4. Things in any room

   skylight _____

   _____

   _____

2 **Circle the item that doesn't belong.**

1. bed   (barbecue)   pillow

2. fireplace   mantle   closet

3. desk   kitchen   chair

4. garden   wall unit   television

5. family room   bedroom   living room

6. old-fashioned modern   expensive

Is There a Swimming Pool?

❶ Circle the correct words.

1. (There is) / There are a family room in our new house.

2. **Is there / Are there** a fireplace in your house?

3. **There was / There were** a skylight in my old house.

4. **There was / There is** a plasma TV in our new living room.

5. **Was there / Were there** mini blinds in your old house?

6. **Is there / Are there** mini blinds in your new house?

7. **There is / There was** a big kitchen in our new house.

8. **Were there / Are there** two windows in your new bedroom?

9. **Was there / Were there** flowers in the garden?

10. **Is there / Are there** trees in your yard?

❷ Complete the sentences about the picture with *is, are, isn't,* or *aren't.*

1. There _____*is*_____ a car near the house.

2. There _____ flowers in the yard.

3. There _____ windows in the house.

4. There _____ a barbecue in the yard.

5. There _____ trees in the yard.

6. There _____ water near the car.

7. There _____ children in the yard.

8. There _____ a garage near the house.

3 Write sentences. Put the words in the correct order.

1. (wall unit / the / big / very / is)

   The wall unit is very big.

2. (bedroom / my / pretty / is / furniture)

   _____

3. (nice / their / view / apartment / has / a)

   _____

4. (three / children / little / were / there / in the yard)

   _____

5. (big / in / is / Anna's / family room / there / a / house)

   _____

6. (sofa / have / they / comfortable / a)

   _____

7. (house / new / has / skylights / big / two / their)

   _____

8. (was / busy / street / a / near / house / my / there)

   _____

9. (apartment / interesting / in / is / the / location / an)

   _____

10. (new / my / neighbors / have / gardens / beautiful)

    _____

4 Complete the following comparisons. Write about yourself.

1. I like _____ better than _____ .

2. I am _____ than my parents.

3. This class is _____ than _____ .

4. English is _____ than my first language.

5. My living room is _____ than _____ .

⑤ Answer the questions about the apartments.

-FOR RENT-

4-bedroom house with 1.5 baths and a family room. No garage. Large yard with barbecue. $$$$

1. The house has two bathrooms.	True	False
2. There is a swimming pool in the yard.	True	False
3. The house is good for a two-car family.	True	False
4. The house is good for people with three children.	True	False
5. The family can cook in the yard.	True	False

-FOR RENT-

One-bedroom apartment with large bath. Sixth floor. Old-fashioned kitchen. Fireplace and skylight in living room. Indoor parking for one car. $$

6. The bathroom is tiny.	True	False
7. The living room is unusual.	True	False
8. The kitchen is modern.	True	False
9. The building has a garage.	True	False
10. This is a good apartment for a large family.	True	False

⑥ Complete the sentences with the words *was, wasn't, were,* or *weren't.*

1. Q: _____Were_____ there a lot of windows in your old apartment?

   A: No, there _____weren't._____

2. Q: _____ your old apartment very big?

   A: Yes, it _____ .

3. Q: _____ your neighbors friendly?

   A: No, they _____ .

4. Q: _____ there mini blinds on the windows?

   A: Yes, there _____ .

5. Q: _____ there a fireplace?

   A: No, there _____ .

6. Q: _____ you happy in the apartment?

   A: No, I _____ .

7. Q: _____ there a TV in the living room?

   A: Yes, there _____ .

8. Q: _____ I ever in your old apartment?

   A: Yes, you _____ .

How Do You Like the Apartment?

1 Match the opposites.

1. new __e__
2. bright _____
3. small _____
4. old-fashioned _____
5. ugly _____
6. tall _____
7. safe _____
8. noisy _____
9. interesting _____

a. quiet
b. short
c. modern
d. dark
e. ~~old~~
f. large
g. pretty
h. boring
i. dangerous

2 Complete the sentences with *too* or *very*.

1. A studio apartment doesn't have any bedrooms.

   It's __too__ small for a family with children.

2. I like to eat at good restaurants. I really love good food.

   But $75 for dinner is _____ expensive for me.

3. The Johnsons have four children. They have a three-bedroom apartment.

   Their apartment is _____ big.

4. Jim's apartment has three bedrooms. He lives there alone.

   It is _____ large for one person.

5. José lives on the 35th floor of a large apartment building in New York City.

   The view from his apartment is _____ good.

6. I like to buy clothes, but I don't have a lot of money. I don't shop at department stores.

   Department store clothes are _____ expensive for me.

7. Bob found a nice apartment on a busy street, but he didn't take it.

   The street was _____ noisy for him. He needs a quiet place to work.

8. I saw a lamp in the store. I didn't really like it.

   But it was _____ cheap so I bought it.

3 Complete the sentences with *is as* + adjective + *as* or *isn't as* + adjective + *as.*

A B C	1. (big) The A *isn't as big as* the B.
	2. (big) The A *is as big as* the C.
④ ⑤ ⑥	3. (small) The five _____ the four.
	4. (small) The six _____ the five.
★ ⏰ →	5. (dark) The star _____ the arrow.
	6. (dark) The clock _____ the arrow.
☎ ✉	7. (large) The letter _____ the telephone.
	8. (large) The telephone_____ the letter.
▲ ▭	9. (tall) The rectangle _____ triangle.
	10. (dark) The rectangle _____ the triangle.
W i	11. (wide) The *i* _____ the *w*.
	12. (dark) The *w* _____ the *i*.

4 Complete the *as . . . as* comparisons. Use *is* and *isn't.*

TV = $500 Stove = $500 End table = $150 Lamp = $150	1. (expensive) The television *is as expensive as* the stove. 2. (expensive) The lamp *isn't as expensive as* the stove. 3. (cheap) The end table _____ the lamp. 4. (cheap) The stove _____ the lamp.
Living Room = 12 ft. × 20 ft Dining room = 12 ft × 12 ft Bedroom = 12 ft × 12 ft	5. (long) The dining room _____ the living room. 6. (small) The living room _____ the dining room. 7. (big) The dining room _____ the bedroom. 8. (small) The living room _____ the bedroom.
Ellen = 5 ft 3 in Mary = 5 ft 6 in Carol = 5 ft 9 in Lisa = 5 ft 6 in	9. (tall) Mary _____ Lisa. 10. (tall) Mary _____ Carol. 11. (short) Lisa _____ Ellen. 12. (short) Lisa _____ Mary.

Call the Manager

Lesson 3

① Match the words that go together.

1. dripping _d_
2. broken ____
3. empty ____
4. professional ____
5. difficult ____
6. clogged ____
7. available ____
8. security ____

a. repair problems
b. apartments
c. deposit
d. ~~faucets~~
e. repair person
f. toilets
g. windows
h. immediately

② Complete the sentences with *too* + adjective or adjective + *enough*.

1. Carol has blond hair and blue eyes. She is a very good-looking young woman.
   Carols friends say she is __beautiful enough__ (beautiful) to be a movie star.

2. This apartment costs $1,500 a month. Ali makes $500 a week at his job.
   The apartment is _____ (expensive) for him.

3. Basketball players must be six feet tall. Jerry is six feet two inches tall.
   Jerry is _____ (tall) to be a basketball player.

4. Apartment 6-E is a one-bedroom apartment. It has a small living room.
   The apartment isn't _____ (big) for a family with children.

5. Linda wears a size eight dress. Her mother also wears a size eight.
   Her mother's dresses are _____ (large) for Linda.

6. The temperature in Miami is warm all year round. I like cold weather in winter.
   Miami is _____ (warm) for me.

7. I like safe sports like riding a bicycle or playing tennis.
   Skiing in the mountains is _____ (dangerous) for me.

8. I don't want to live in New York City. The people there are not very friendly.
   The people in New York City are not _____ (friendly) for me.

34 Housing

③ Circle the correct words.

–FOR RENT–

One-bedroom apartment – Tenth floor – Lovely living room – lots of windows – Very clean – just painted – $900 a month

Bob makes $900 a week. He is married and has four children. He could walk from the apartment to his job in ten minutes. There is a beautiful view from the living room window. The apartment is very clean. They could move in today.

1. The apartment is **cheap enough** / **too cheap**.
2. It is **too small / small enough** for six people.
3. The apartment is **too close / close enough** to Bob's job.
4. It is **clean enough / too clean.**
5. The apartment is **high enough / too high** to have good views.

–FOR RENT–

Three-bedroom house – Built in 1930 – Very friendly neighborhood. Near all transportation – $1,200 a month

Linda is married and has two children. She can pay up to $1,500 a month. She wants to live in a new house so there aren't any repairs. The street isn't very quiet. Linda doesn't want to live in a noisy neighborhood.

6. The house is **too old / old enough** for Linda.
7. It is **too big / big enough** for Linda's family.
8. The street is **too noisy / noisy enough** for Linda.
9. The house is **too cheap / cheap enough.**
10. The neighborhood is **too friendly / friendly enough.**

④ Match each word with the correct definition.

1. utilities __b__
2. security deposit _____
3. sublet _____
4. term _____
5. tenant _____
6. date of occupancy _____

a. how long the contract lasts
b. gas and electricity
c. person who lives in the apartment
d. rent to someone else
e. money you pay before you move in
f. when a person moves into an apartment

Review

① Bubble the correct answers.

                                                           a b c

1. There _____ a party at Mike's house last week.
   a) is   b) isn't   c) was   ◯ ◯ ◯

2. They live in a _____ .
   a) very small house   b) small house very   c) house very small   ◯ ◯ ◯

3. Rita's baby is _____ than Gail's baby.
   a) more tiny   b) tinyer   c) tinier   ◯ ◯ ◯

4. The chair is _____ than the sofa.
   a) as comfortable   b) not comfortable   c) less comfortable   ◯ ◯ ◯

5. The _____ collects the rent.
   a) manager   b) tenant   c) repair person   ◯ ◯ ◯

② Read the story. Circle the correct answers.

> ### Rita's New Apartment
>
>   Rita wants to move to a smaller apartment and pay less rent. Right now she pays $850 a month and she wants to save $150 a month. Rita saw a nice apartment last week. It had one bedroom and a big kitchen, but the view wasn't good at all. The view is really important to her.
>
>   Yesterday Rita saw a really unusual apartment. It has one bedroom and a small living room with a fireplace. There is also a small dining room next to the kitchen. It's on the first floor and she can use the garden. It's the same size as her old apartment, and the rent is $800 a month. She wants to pay less. But it is more comfortable than her present apartment, and the garden is so beautiful.

1. Rita wants **a large /(a smaller)** apartment.

2. She wants to pay **$700 / $600** a month.

3. She saw an apartment with **one bedroom / a nice view** last week.

4. Yesterday she saw **an old-fashioned / an unusual** apartment.

5. The apartment had a nice **garden / bathroom.**

6. It also has **a nice view / a fireplace** .

7. The new apartment **is as big as / isn't as big as** her old apartment.

8. The new apartment is **more expensive than / less expensive than** the old one.

The Past

Chapter 5

Vocabulary

① What did Cindy do yesterday? Complete the sentences.

1. Cindy had a busy day __h__ .
2. She got up at _____.
3. Then she took _____.
4. She wanted _____.
5. Alberto called her on the telephone and they _____.
6. Cindy drank a _____.
7. After that, Cindy's neighbor wanted to _____.
8. They ate lunch _____.
9. Cindy rested for a while after she got _____.
10. She cooked dinner in the evening, but _____.

a. talked for a long time
b. go shopping
c. home
d. a shower
e. 7:00
f. she didn't clean the apartment
g. to clean the apartment
h. ~~yesterday~~
i. at a small café
j. cup of coffee

② Complete the sentences with words from the box.

baseball player	plumber	mechanic	receptionist	~~nurse~~
child-care worker	waiter	gardener	math teacher	jockey

1. A ____nurse____ takes care of sick people.
2. A _____ repairs toilets and sinks.
3. A _____ fixes cars.
4. A _____ takes orders and serves food.
5. A _____ cuts the grass.
6. A _____ runs around the bases.
7. A _____ greets people and answers the telephone.
8. A _____ teaches people about numbers.
9. A _____ rides race horses.
10. A _____ takes care of little children.

How Was Your Day?

1 Choose the correct past tense form.

1. I **listened** / **listenned** to the teacher.
2. The baby **cryed** / **cried** for an hour.
3. We **shoped** / **shopped** for food at the supermarket.
4. He **droped** / **dropped** the soccer ball.
5. We **studyed** / **studied** for two hours.
6. They **played** / **plaied** tennis all morning.
7. Ellen **cooked** / **cookd** dinner for her family.
8. He **tried** / **tryed** to speak Spanish.
9. They **startid** / **started** work at 8:00.
10. Jim **carryed** / **carried** the groceries home.

2 Choose the correct pronunciation.

	/t/ /d/ /id/		/t/ /d/ /id/
1. cleaned	○ ○ ○	6. needed	○ ○ ○
2. worked	○ ○ ○	7. baked	○ ○ ○
3. rested	○ ○ ○	8. walked	○ ○ ○
4. called	○ ○ ○	9. smiled	○ ○ ○
5. wanted	○ ○ ○	10. cleaned	○ ○ ○

3 Complete the following sentences. Write about yourself or a friend.

1. _____ an hour ago.
2. _____ yesterday afternoon.
3. _____ last night.
4. _____ last week.
5. _____ five years ago.

4 Complete the sentences with the correct past tense form.

1. My friends and I _____wanted_____ (want) to see the concert.

2. We _____ (carry) our blankets to the beach.

3. We _____ (drop) them near the band.

4. Then we _____ (rest) for a while.

5. The band _____ (start) at 7:00.

6. They _____ (play) loud music for several hours.

7. We _____ (listen) and _____ (dance).

8. They _____ (stop) at midnight.

5 Complete each sentence with *last*, *ago*, or *yesterday*.

1. We painted the living room _____yesterday_____ .

2. I visited my family _____ month.

3. Frank played soccer _____ afternoon.

4. We washed the windows two months _____ .

5. I talked to Lin the day before _____ .

6. We studied _____ night.

7. I didn't eat breakfast _____ morning.

8. Anna called her mother _____ Friday.

9. Class started an hour _____ .

10. Mary danced for hours _____ evening.

Yesterday

1 Write questions. Put the words in order.

1. (English / study / where / you / did)
   Where did you study English?

2. (did / learn / what / yesterday / you)
   _____

3. (buy / your / you / did / car / where)
   _____

4. (eat / what / you / for / breakfast / did)
   _____

5. (they / where / sleep / last / did / night)
   _____

6. (yesterday / wear / evening / did / what / she)
   _____

7. (meet / your / where / husband / did / you)
   _____

8. (supermarket / buy / at the / you / what / did)
   _____

9. (muffin / where / that / get / you / did)
   _____

10. (breakfast / with / you / did / drink / what)
   _____

2 Read the answers. Write the questions.

1. Q: *What time did he start work yesterday morning?*
   A: He started work at 8:00 yesterday morning.

2. Q: _____
   A: They found muffins in the box.

3. Q: _____
   A: They saw the receptionist in the office.

4. Q: _____
   A: He went home at 10:00.

5. Q: _____
   A: She bought the groceries at Lim's.

6. Q: _____
   A: He used the computer in the morning.

7. Q: _____
   A: She got up at 6:30.

8. Q: _____
   A: I wrote to my grandmother.

9. Q: _____
   A: They grew onions and beans in their garden.

10. Q: _____
   A: I won a new car.

40   The Past

❸ Complete the sentences. Use the past tense.

1. I go to the movies every Friday.

   I went to the movies _____ last Friday.

2. She brings her dictionary every day.

   _____ yesterday.

3. They buy a new car every year.

   _____ last year.

4. I cut my hair every month.

   _____ last month.

5. I drink coffee every morning.

   _____ this morning.

6. They drive to work every day.

   _____ last Monday.

7. We leave at 7:00 every day.

   _____ this morning.

8. He pays the health club $15 every week.

   _____ last week.

9. I ride my bicycle every weekend.

   _____ last Sunday.

10. We run every morning.

   _____ yesterday morning.

❹ Read the schedule. Complete the sentences. Tell what Linda did yesterday.

8 A.M.	get up	12 P.M.	take a break
9 A.M.	leave the house	1 P.M.	eat lunch
10 A.M.	arrive at school	2 P.M.	go to the library

1. Linda _got up at 8:00_ _____ .

2. She _____ .

3. She _____ .

4. Linda _____ .

5. She _____ .

6. She _____ .

⑤ Complete the questions and answers.

1. Q: Where did he _____buy_____ that shirt? (buy)

   A: He _____bought_____ it at Ron's Menswear.

2. Q: Did he _____ it to class yesterday? (wear)

   A: No, he didn't. He _____ his green shirt.

3. Q: Did you _____ eight hours last night? (sleep)

   A: No, I _____ five hours.

4. Q: Did your daughter _____ a picture of you? (draw)

   A: No, she _____ a picture of her aunt.

5. Q: Where did you _____ Annie? (meet)

   A: I _____ her at a dance.

6. Q: When did you _____ the letter? (send)

   A: I _____ it yesterday morning.

7. Q: Did Carlos _____ work on Friday? (begin)

   A: No, he _____ work on Monday.

8. Q: Did your mother _____ these cookies? (make)

   A: No, my father _____ them.

⑥ Complete the conversations.

1. A: Where did you _____go_____ after class? (go)

   B: I _____went_____ to the library. (go)

   A: Did you _____ magazines? (read)

   B: No, I _____ a letter. (write)

2. A: What did they _____ yesterday morning? (do)

   B: They _____ their bicycles. (ride)

   A: Where did they _____? (go)

   B: They _____ to Alpine Park. (go)

3. A: Did you _____ your sister last night? (see)

   B: No, but I _____ to her on the phone. (speak)

   A: When did you _____ her? (call)

   B: I _____ to her around 9:00. (speak)

What Did You Do on That Job?

1 Complete the conversations.

1. **receptionist**   **answer telephones**   **greet people**

A: What was her last job?

B: *She was a receptionist.*

A: What did she do on that job?

B: *She answered telephones and greeted people.*

2. *nurse*   *take care of sick people*

A: What did he do in 2001?

B: _____

A: What did he do on that job?

B: _____

3. **waitress**   **take food orders**   **serve food**

A: What was her first job?

B: _____

A: What did she do on that job?

B: _____

4. plumber   repair sinks and toilets

A: What was her last job?

B: _____

A: What did she do on that job?

B: _____

5. *gardener*   *cut the grass*   *grow flowers*

A: What did your uncle do?

B: _____

A: What did he do on that job?

B: _____

6. *child-care worker*   *take care of children*   *read them stories*

A: What was Anna's last job?

B: _____

A: What did she do on that job?

B: _____ .

2 Read the chart. Answer the questions about Sam in complete sentences. Use *ago* in your answers.

1975	1997	1998	1999	2001	2003	2004	NOW (2005)
Born	Move to the U.S.	English classes	First job (waiter)	Second job (cook)	Meet Linda	Third job (Manager)	Marry Linda

1. When was Sam born? *He was born 30 years ago.*

2. When did he move to the U.S.? _____

3. When did he begin English classes? _____

4. When did he get his first job? _____

5. When did he become a cook? _____

6. When did he meet Linda? _____

7. When did he become a manager? _____

3 Look at the chart in 2 above. Answer the questions about Sam. Use complete sentences.

1. How old is Sam now?
   He is 30 years old.

2. How old was he when he moved to the U.S.?

   _____

3. How old was he when he got his first job?

   _____

4. How long did he work as a waiter?

   _____

5. How long did he work as a cook?

   _____

6. How long did he live in the U.S. before he met Linda?

   _____

7. How long did he know Linda before he married her?

   _____

8. How old was he when he became a manager?

   _____

Review

1 Bubble the correct answers.

a b c

1. They _____ the garage on Saturday.
   a) washed   b) cleaned out   c) drove   ○ ○ ○

2. She _____ to the children last night.
   a) sings   b) singed   c) sang   ○ ○ ○

3. They _____ to church on Sunday.
   a) went   b) were   c) took   ○ ○ ○

4. We saw that movie _____ week.
   a) ago   b) before   c) last   ○ ○ ○

5. I _____ you an e-mail last week.
   a) sended   b) sent   c) send   ○ ○ ○

2 Read Brenda's story. Answer the questions. Use complete sentences.

Interesting Jobs

Many students get jobs to make money while they attend school. Lisa was an art major in college. She got a job as a receptionist in an art gallery. She saw a lot of unusual paintings and met a lot of interesting people. Lisa told her friends, "Someday my paintings will be in a gallery like this."

Joe worked as a gardener when he was in college. They paid him $15 an hour so he made almost $1,000 a month. He bought books and paid for his food with the money. Sometimes he cut flowers and brought them to his friends. The manager said it was OK. There were plenty of flowers in the gardens.

Susan was in a teacher-training program at her college. She had a part-time job as a child-care worker. Most days she read the children stories and gave them snacks. Sometimes she brought her guitar to class and played it for them. On Fridays they went to the beach. They swam and played games near the water. After working there for a year, Susan knew for sure that she wanted to be a teacher.

1. What was Lisa's job? _She was a receptionist in an art gallery._____

2. What kind of people did Lisa meet? _____

3. How much did they pay Joe? _____

4. What did Joe bring to his friends? _____

5. What did Susan sometimes bring to class? _____

6. What did Susan want to be? _____

Critical Thinking

7. Which job would you like? Give reasons for your answer. _____

Free Time

Chapter 6

Vocabulary

1 Label each activity.

| W = warm-weather activity | C = cold-weather activity | A = any-weather activity |

1. __W__ bike riding
2. _____ sailing
3. _____ shopping
4. _____ ice skating

5. _____ water skiing
6. _____ hiking
7. _____ swimming

8. _____ dancing
9. _____ snow skiing
10. _____ camping

2 Match the event with the correct month.

1. Summer begins in ___e___ .
2. Valentine's Day is in _____ .
3. Thanksgiving is in _____ .
4. Spring begins in _____ .
5. Memorial Day is in _____ .
6. Winter begins in _____ .
7. Fall begins in _____ .
8. New Year's Day is in _____ .
9. Independence Day is in _____ .
10. Halloween is in _____ .

a. January
b. February
c. March
d. May
e. ~~June~~
f. July
g. September
h. October
i. November
j. December

3 Fill in the blank with *play, go,* or *take.*

1. ___go___ jogging
2. _____ photographs
3. _____ cards

4. _____ baseball
5. _____ dancing
6. _____ windowshopping

How Was Your Vacation?

1 Complete the conversations.

1. A: _Where did you go_ on Saturday? (go)

   B: We went to the park.

   A: What _did you do_ ? (do)

   B: We _went jogging_
      and _had a picnic_ . (jogging, a picnic)

   A: Did you _go swimming?_ (swimming)

   B: No, we didn't.

2. A: _____ your weekend? (be)

   B: It was great.

   A: Where _____ ? (go)

   B: I _____ anywhere. I
      _____ here. (go, stay)

   A: _____ ? (shopping)

   B: I _____ , but I didn't buy
      anything. (window-shopping)

3. A: _____ your vacation? (be)

   B: It was cold.

   A: What _____ ? (do)

   B: We _____ . (skiing)

   A: Did you _____ ? (photographs)

   B: Yes, we did. We took a lot.

4. A: What _____ last week? (do)

   B: We _____ . (hiking)

   A: Where _____ ? (go)

   B: We went to Yosemite.

   A: _____ ? (horses)

   B: No, but we _____ . (some souvenirs)

5. A: _____ your vacation? (be)

   B: It was fun.

   A: Who _____ ? (visit)

   B: We visited my aunt in New York City.

   A: Did you _____ ? (sightseeing)

   B: No, but we _____ every day.
      (shopping)

6. A: _____ your trip to Chicago? (be)

   B: It was very unusual.

   A: How long _____ ? (stay)

   B: For a week.

   A: _____ ? (eat in good restaurants)

   B: No, but we _____ every night.
      (dancing)

2 Fix the mistakes in the incorrect sentences. If the sentence is correct, write *correct*.

1. Q: Did he came to school yesterday?
   A: Yes, he did.

2. Q: Did you watch the news last night?
   A: No, I didn't watched it.

3. Q: Did they going swimming?
   A: Yes, they did.

4. Q: Did he cut his hair?
   A: Yes, he did. He cutted his hair last week.

5. Q: Did you took any photographs?
   A: No, I didn't.

6. Q: Did Judy go skiing last week?
   A: Yes, she went.

7. Q: Did you went horseback riding?
   A: No, I didn't not.

8. Q: Did you heard the answer?
   A: Yes, I did.

1. Q: *Did he come to school yesterday?*
   A: *Correct*

2. Q: _____
   A: _____

3. Q: _____
   A: _____

4. Q: _____
   A: _____

5. Q: _____
   A: _____

6. Q: _____
   A: _____

7. Q: _____
   A: _____

8. Q: _____
   A: _____

3 Write questions. Put the words in order.

1. (dancing / like / you / would / go / to)
   Would you like to go dancing?

2. (he / go / like / would / camping / to)
   _____

3. (she / to / go / skating / ice / would / like)
   _____

4. (would / like / the children / to / horseback riding / go)
   _____

5. (play / brother / your / like / would / to / cards)
   _____

4 Write past tense statements about Alberto's vacation.

1. How was your vacation?   (be / great)

   <u>It was great.</u>

2. Where did you go?   (go / Miami Beach)

   _____

3. How long did you stay?   (stay / two weeks)

   _____

4. How did you get there?   (fly / from New York City)

   _____

5. What did you eat?   (a lot of oranges and bananas)

   _____

6. When did you go?   (go / last month)

   _____

7. What did you do there?   (go / swimming and water skiing)

   _____

8. Did you see any interesting buildings?   (Yes / go sightseeing one day)

   _____

9. Did you take any photographs?   (yes)

   _____

10. What did you buy?   (buy / some souvenirs)

   _____

5 Complete the sentences with *and* or *but*.

1. I went hiking, <u> but </u> my friends didn't go hiking.

2. Lisa often goes camping, _____ Tim often goes camping, too.

3. They play soccer, _____ they also go jogging, too.

4. I like to sunbathe at the beach, _____ I don't like to go swimming.

5. Carlos rides a bicycle, _____ he also rides a horse.

6. We didn't eat in a restaurant, _____ we had a picnic.

How Was the Weather?

❶ Describe the weather in your city.

1. What season of the year is it right now?

   _____

2. What was the high temperature yesterday?

   _____

3. What was the low temperature?

   _____

4. Was it sunny or cloudy?

   _____

5. What was the weather like?

   _____

6. What is the weather like today?

   _____

❷ Circle the correct word.

1. It's sunny in San Diego. The weather is **beautiful** / awful.

2. It's cold and rainy in New York. The weather is **nice / terrible**.

3. The temperature is 40 degrees in Miami. It's **cold / hot**.

4. It's windy and rainy in San Francisco. The weather is **good / bad**.

5. It's summer in Dallas. The weather is **hot / snowy**.

6. It's warm and sunny in Atlanta. The weather is **great / terrible**.

7. It's 105 degrees in New York City. The weather is **awful / nice**.

8. It's winter in Chicago. The weather is **cold / hot**.

9. It's 30 degrees and windy in Chicago. The weather is **bad / beautiful**.

10. It's spring in Washington, DC. The weather is **awful / nice**.

3 Answer the questions about the weather map. Use complete sentences.

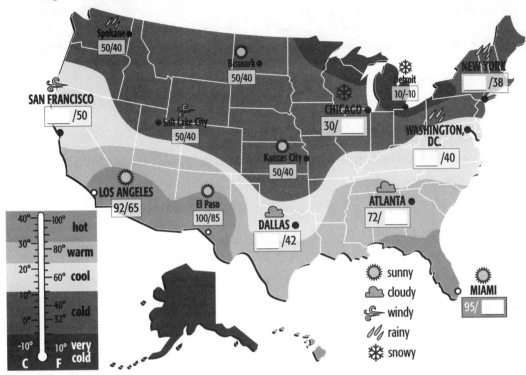

1. What was the high temperature in Detroit? ___It was 10 degrees.___

2. What was the weather like in El Paso? _____

3. What was the low temperature in Los Angeles? _____

4. How was the weather in Washington, DC.? _____

5. What was the high temperature in Bismark? _____

6. What was the weather like in Dallas? _____

7. What was the low temperature in Kansas City? _____

8. How was the weather in New York? _____

4 Complete the questions and answers. Use the correct past form of *do* or *be*.

1. Q: _____Did_____ you have a nice vacation?

   A: Yes, we did.

2. Q: Was the weather good?

   A: No, it _____ .

3. Q: Were the restaurants good?

   A: Yes, they _____ .

4. Q: Were you happy with the hotel?

   A: No, I _____ .

5. Q: Did Rosa buy a lot of souvenirs?

   A: Yes, she _____ .

6. Q: Was the weather hot?

   A: Yes, it _____ .

7. Q: Did you go jogging?

   A: No, we _____ .

8. Q: Were the people friendly?

   A: No, they _____ .

I Work at a Travel Agency

① Put the conversations in order. Write numbers.

1. _____ Yes, it does.

   __1__ Hi. This is Arnie. How can I help you?

   _____ Yes, we do. We have a three-night special at the Desert Hotel for $300.

   _____ Does that include airfare?

   __2__ I'm interested in going to Las Vegas. Do you have any specials?

2. _____ It's $150 a night per person.

   _____ Yes, please. I'd like to visit Orlando, Florida, for a week. Do you have any specials?

   _____ Yes, there's a 10 percent discount on the Orlando Inn until June 1.

   _____ Timon's Travel Agency. May I help you?

   _____ How much is it?

   _____ That sounds great. I'd like to book it.

3. _____ Yes, it does.

   _____ This is Debbie at Holidays Unlimited.

   _____ Yes, there's a one-week special at the Darrison Hotel for $200 a person.

   _____ Does it include a rental car?

   _____ Let's book it.

   _____ I'm interested in visiting Chicago. Do you have any specials?

4. _____ Yes, we do. There's a five-night special in Cancun for $200 a person.

   _____ Do you have any discounts on vacations in Mexico?

   _____ Does it include sightseeing and fishing trips?

   _____ Time Travel. Sam speaking.

   _____ Yes, it does.

5. _____ We have a one-week special that includes the hotel and all meals for $795 a person.

   _____ I'm interested in visiting the Grand Canyon this spring.

   _____ Arizona Adventures. How can I help you?

   _____ Are there any discounts?

   _____ Yes, there's a 20 percent discount if you book before January 1.

6. _____ My parents want to visit me here in Seattle next month.

   _____ No, it doesn't.

   _____ Well, we have a special at the Wonder Hotel for $400 a person for the week of April 9–15.

   _____ Hello. This is Mike. How can I help you?

   _____ Does that include airfare?

❷ Complete the sentences about scheduled events in the future. Use the present tense.

1. Q: What time _does the bus leave_ ?   (bus / leave)

   A: It _____ leaves _____ at 6:00 tonight.

2. Q: When _____ ?   (concert / begin)

   A: It _____ at 9 P.M.

3. Q: When _____ ?   (one-week special / end)

   A: It _____ next Monday.

4. Q: When _____ ?   (your cousin / get here)

   A: He _____ tomorrow at noon.

5. Q: What time _____ tomorrow?   (test / start)

   A: It _____ at 3:00.

6. Q: When _____ ?   (the bus / arrive)

   A: It _____ at 5 P.M.

7. Q: What time _____ ?   (the train / depart)

   A: It _____ at 8:00.

8. Q: When _____ ?   (your vacation / end)

   A: It _____ on Monday.

❸ Read the sentences. Fill in the missing information in the train schedule.

DAY TRIPPER 1		DAY TRIPPER 2	
Rochester to New York City $55 One Way _____ Round Trip		Rochester to New York City _____ One Way $75 Round Trip	
Departs Rochester	8:00 A.M.	Departs Rochester	7:00 A.M.
Arrives Buffalo	_____	Arrives Buffalo	_____
Departs Buffalo	11:00 A.M.	Departs Buffalo	12:00 P.M.
Arrives New York City	_____	Arrives New York City	8:00 P.M.

1. The Day Tripper 2 leaves Buffalo at 12:00 P.M.

2. The Day Tripper 1 gets to Buffalo at 10:00 A.M.

3. The one-way fare on the Day Tripper 2 is $40.

4. The round-trip fare on the Day Tripper 1 is $100.

5. The Day Tripper 1 arrives in New York at 5:00 P.M.

6. The Day Tripper 2 arrives in Buffalo at 11:00 A.M.

❶ Bubble the correct answers.

a b c

1. _____ is a summer holiday.

   a) Independence Day   b) Thanksgiving   c) Valentine's Day   ○ ○ ○

2. You need snow to _____ .

   a) go sailing   b) go skiing   c) go hiking   ○ ○ ○

3. In college, many students _____ a sport.

   a) play   b) take   c) go   ○ ○ ○

4. I like vacations, _____ I don't like sightseeing.

   a) how   b) and   c) but   ○ ○ ○

5. They go _____ a lot in the summer.

   a) swim   b) swimming   c) to swim   ○ ○ ○

6. _____ you at home last night?

   a) Are   b) Did   c) Were   ○ ○ ○

❷ Read the story. Fill in the missing verbs.

A Great Trip

My friend Linda and her husband, Dick, live in New York City. They _took_ a great vacation last year. They didn't have a lot of money, but they _wanted_ to _visit_ Florida. They _____ to a travel agent. She _____ a three-night special at a beachfront hotel for only $400 a person. It didn't _____ airfare, but there _____ a 10 percent discount if they _____ the trip before February 1. They _____ "Yes" right away.

They _____ the airport in New York at 9:00 A.M. and _____ in Miami at 11:00. They _____ to the hotel and _____ lunch. Then they _____ swimming at the beach. Dick _____ a lot of photographs. That evening they _____ dinner in a fancy restaurant and _____ dancing. They didn't _____ home until midnight.

The next day they _____ to take a day trip. In the morning they _____ hiking in the Everglades. At noon, they _____ a picnic in the park. In the afternoon, they _____ fishing. Linda _____ three fish, but Dick didn't _____ any. Before dinner, they _____ water skiing. They both _____ in the water a few times, but they _____ a great time. That night they _____ ten hours! They didn't _____ up until noon. They both _____ it _____ the best vacation ever.

Shopping

Vocabulary

1 **Complete the lists with words from the box. Use each word once.**

~~tennis racquet~~	earrings	radio	necklace
sofa	~~CD player~~	~~watch~~	~~lamp~~
bicycle	running shoes	chair	computer
television	skis	bracelet	table

1. Sporting goods

   tennis racquet _____

   _____

   _____

   _____

2. Jewelry

   watch _____

   _____

   _____

   _____

3. Electronics

   CD player _____

   _____

   _____

   _____

4. Furniture

   lamp _____

   _____

   _____

   _____

2 **Circle the item that doesn't belong.**

1. shirt   (shoe)   button

2. delicious   expensive   cheap

3. housewares   pots and pans   clothes

4. shirt   men's department cake

5. a refund   a store credit a big sale

6. sweater   perfume   cosmetics

Where Can I Find the Pots and Pans?

1 **Answer the questions. Use the words *front, back, left,* and *right*.**

D

A   C

B

1. Where's A? *It's on the left.*
2. Where's B? _____
3. Where's C? _____
4. Where's D? _____

2 **Complete the sentences. Use the future tense with *will* or *won't*.**

1. I eat dinner at home every day.

   I will eat dinner at home _____ this evening.

2. She wrote a long letter yesterday.

   _____ tomorrow.

3. They study together every weekend.

   _____ next weekend.

4. We watched the soccer game on TV last week.

   _____ next week.

5. I don't go to bed early.

   _____ tonight.

6. He didn't do his homework yesterday.

   _____ tomorrow.

3 **Complete the questions and answers. Use the future tense.**

1. Q: _____*Will*_____ they _____*arrive*_____ tomorrow? (arrive)

   A: No, ___*they won't*___ .

2. Q: _____ they _____ next week? (finish school)

   A: Yes, _____ .

3. Q: _____ she _____ next week? (return)

   A: No, _____ .

4. Q: _____ you _____ this evening? (stay home)

   A: Yes, I _____ .

4 Ask and answer questions about what people will buy. Use *How many ... ?*

What gifts will students buy for their friends this year?														
Clothing														14
Jewelry										10				
Electronics								8						
Sporting goods						6								
Appliances				4										
Toys			3											

1. Q: *How many students will buy clothing?*

   A: *Fourteen students will buy clothing.*

2. Q: _____

   A: _____

3. Q: _____

   A: _____

4. Q: _____

   A: _____

5. Q: _____

   A: _____

6. Q: _____

   A: _____

5 Make some predictions about your life.

1. What will you get for your birthday?

   _____

2. What time will you go to bed tonight?

   _____

3. How many movies will you see this year?

   _____

4. When will you buy a new car?

   _____

5. What grade will you get in this class?

   _____

I Might Buy Earrings

1 Complete the chart.

Adjective	Comparative	Superlative
1. good	better	best
2. funny		
3. small		
4. delicious		
5. bad		
6. nice		
7. amazing		
8. far		
9. big		
10. cheap		

2 Circle the correct words.

1. A: What can I do for you?

   B: I want a **most delicious /
   (really delicious)** cake.

   A: This is the **better / best** one.

   B: OK. I'll take it.

2. A: Do you like the sofa or the chair?

   B: I like the sofa. It's **more comfortable
   / most comfortable.**

   A: Is the sofa expensive?

   B: Yes, it's **more expensive /
   most expensive** than the chair.

3. A: Is Nero's restaurant **good / better**
   than Henry's?

   B: I think so. I think Nero's is **the better /
   the best** restaurant in town.

4. A: Who lives **the farther / the farthest**
   from the school?

   B: I think I do. I live four miles away.

   A: Does anyone live **far / farther**
   than that?

   C: I do. I live six miles away.

5. A: I think this is **the nice / the nicest**
   room in the school.

   B: Why?

   A: Well, the windows are **bigger / biggest**
   than in the other rooms.

   B: That's true. And it has **the better / the
   best** chairs.

6. A: Did you like the movie?

   B: No, but it was **interesting / more
   interesting** than the book.

   A: What was the book like?

   B: It was the **popular / most popular**
   book in the library.

3 Bubble the correct answers.

	a	b	c

1. Houses are _____ than apartments.
   a) expensiver   b) more expensive   c) most expensive   ○ ○ ○

2. Pizza is _____ lunch.
   a) the cheapest   b) a cheapest   c) cheap   ○ ○ ○

3. This garden is _____ than my garden.
   a) more pretty   b) prettyer   c) prettier   ○ ○ ○

4. This is the _____ TV in the store.
   a) bigger   b) bigest   c) biggest   ○ ○ ○

5. Which TV has the _____ picture?
   a) good   b) best   c) gooder   ○ ○ ○

6. Main Street is the _____ street in town.
   a) dirtiest   b) dirtyest   c) most dirty   ○ ○ ○

7. Linda has a _____ job than Karen.
   a) most boring   b) more boring   c) boringer   ○ ○ ○

8. Who has the _____ problems with money?
   a) bad   b) worse   c) worst   ○ ○ ○

4 Complete the sentences with *might, may,* or *will.*

1. I'm not sure. I _might (may)_ go to the library after school.
2. I _____ be at the bus station at 6:00. Meet me there.
3. I don't know yet. I _____ go to the movies tonight.
4. They don't know for sure. It _____ snow tonight.
5. She is always on time. She _____ be here by 3:00.
6. This class _____ end in June.

⑤ Circle the correct words.

1. A: Are you going to buy the black car?

   B: I **will buy /** (**might buy**) it. What do you think?

   A: I'd buy the white car. It's **reliabler / more reliable.**

2. A: This is a great clothing store. What are you going to buy?

   B: I'm not sure. I **will buy / may buy** a new suit.

   A: I think you should buy your suit at Gracy's.

   B: Why?

   A: Their prices are **more low / lower.**

3. A: Is this store open until 9:00?

   B: No, it **may close / will close** at 6:00.

   A: Should I buy my CDs here?

   B: No. I'd go to Amazing Audio. It's a **more good / better** store.

4. A: Where are you going after lunch?

   B: I **will study / might study** or I **may go / will go** to a movie. I'm not sure.

   A: Go to a movie. It's **the most interesting / more interesting** than studying.

⑥ Fix the mistakes in the incorrect sentences. If the sentence is correct, write *correct.*

1. They won't probably be home this evening.

   They probably won't be home this evening.

2. He'll come probably to class.

   _____

3. She probably will leave by noon.

   _____

4. I probably won't buy a new car this year.

   _____

Customer Service

❶ Complete the sentences.

1. My employer is __g__ .
2. My occupation is _____ .
3. My phone number is _____ .
4. My length of employment is _____ .
5. My monthly salary is _____ .
6. My reference is _____ .
7. My home address is _____ .
8. My zip code is _____ .
9. My account type is _____ .
10. My date of birth is _____ .

a. 10/28/1971
b. 10064
c. Mr. Frank Falco
d. two years
e. $1500
f. salesperson
g. ~~David's Discount Store~~
h. checking
i. 20 Forest Avenue
j. 343-1758

❷ Put the conversations in order. Write numbers.

1. _____ There's a stain on it.
   __1__ I'd like to return this shirt.
   _____ No, thanks. I'd like a refund.
   __2__ What's wrong with it?
   _____ Would you like to exchange it?

2. _____ It doesn't work. I can't turn it on.
   _____ There's something wrong with this TV.
   _____ What's wrong with it?
   _____ Then I'd like to exchange it.
   _____ I can't give you a refund.

3. _____ The zipper is broken.
   _____ Yes, I did.
   _____ Can I return these pants?
   _____ Then I can't give you a refund.
   _____ Sure. What's wrong with them?
   _____ Did you buy them on sale?
   _____ That's OK. I'll take store credit.

3 Complete the sentences. Use a word from the box.

size	it	on	ugly	~~them~~	broken	sleeve	fit	loose	work

1. I can't walk in ___them___ .
2. The computer doesn't _____ .
3. They look _____ .
4. There's a stain on the _____ .
5. It's the wrong _____ .
6. The heels are _____ .
7. I can't close _____ .
8. I can't turn it _____ .
9. It doesn't _____ .
10. The zipper is _____ .

4 Read the ad and answer the questions.

Big Jewelry Sale! This Weekend Only	
DIAMOND BRACELET	**DIAMOND EARRINGS**
Regularly $500	*25% off*
Half off	Now only $300

1. What is the usual cost of the bracelet? ___$500___
2. How long is the sale? _____
3. How much is the discount on the bracelet? _____
4. How much do you save if you buy the bracelet now? _____

5. What is the regular price of the earrings? _____
6. What is the sale price of the earrings? _____
7. How much will you pay for the earrings next week? _____
8. How much do you save if you buy the earrings now? _____

5 Circle True or False.

1. You find running shoes in the housewares department.   True   (False)
2. "Half off" is the same as "a 50 percent discount."   True   False
3. You might buy a computer in the electronics department.   True   False
4. "May" means the same as "might."   True   False
5. A bank manages money.   True   False
6. The word "probably" means that a future action is certain.   True   False
7. Cosmetics include perfume and soap.   True   False
8. When you get an "exchange," you get your money back.   True   False
9. You can buy a refrigerator in the furniture department.   True   False
10. Reduced prices are lower than regular prices.   True   False

Review

1 **Read the story. Bubble the correct answers.**

Making Shopping Easier

Large stores are doing a lot of different things to try to attract more shoppers. Many of them now have greeters who stand near the entrance. The greeters' job is to say hello to the customers as they enter and make them feel at home. They also offer to help people find what they are looking for and answer any other questions customers may have. College students often take jobs as greeters. The position doesn't pay a lot, but it doesn't require long hours or heavy responsibilities. Greeters have the time and energy to do other things—like study.

Discount programs are also a way stores attract shoppers. In addition to the usual 10 percent off coupons, some stores now offer additional discounts if a shopper spends a certain amount of money. For example, the customer may get 20 percent off on the first $100 he or she spends. When the customer spends over $100, the discount may rise to 25 percent. This encourages shoppers to spend more than usual and to buy things at this store instead of another one.

Most large stores also offer online shopping in addition to in-store shopping. Many people find this a very convenient way to shop. It becomes especially important during holiday seasons when shoppers crowd the stores. For many people, it's much more pleasant to sit at home with a cup of coffee and pick out what you want. To make online shopping even more attractive, most stores offer many items at prices that are lower than store prices. Some people think that one day most store buildings will close and we'll do all our shopping on the Internet.

			a	b
1. Many greeters are			○	○
a) full-time employees.	b) college students.			
2. Greeters			○	○
a) are salespeople.	b) say hello to people.			
3. Greeters have			○	○
a) heavy responsibilities.	b) free time.			
4. The usual discount coupon is for			○	○
a) 10 percent off.	b) 20 percent off.			
5. When a customer spends less than $100, the discount is			○	○
a) 20 percent.	b) 25 percent.			
6. Discounts for spending more than $100 encourage customers			○	○
a) to spend less than usual.	b) to spend more than usual.			
7. Prices on the Internet are often			○	○
a) lower than store prices.	b) higher than store prices.			
8. During the holiday season, many people find it more convenient to shop			○	○
a) in stores.	b) online.			

Health and Safety

Chapter 8

Vocabulary

1 Complete the sentences.

1. After the accident I had to wear a neck __c__ .
2. You should always obey safety _____ .
3. José is an emergency medical _____ .
4. The nurse took my blood _____ .
5. In winter I often have a sore _____ .
6. The sign said, "No _____ ."
7. On the way to work, Jill got a speeding _____ .
8. The police officer completed an accident _____ .
9. The skater slipped and _____ .
10. I read the list of active _____ .

a. fell
b. Smoking
c. ~~brace~~
d. technician
e. rules
f. ingredients
g. report
h. pressure
i. ticket
j. throat

2 Label each part of the body.

H = part of the head	A = part of the arm	L = part of the leg

1. __A__ shoulder
2. _____ mouth
3. _____ ankle
4. _____ elbow
5. _____ earlobe
6. _____ eyebrow

7. _____ nose
8. _____ calf
9. _____ wrist
10. _____ forehead
11. _____ knee
12. _____ teeth

What's the Problem?

❶ Circle the correct word.

1. I was at the beach yesterday. Today I have a **bloody /** (**sunburned**) back.
2. I fell over my child's toys. I have a **sprained / black** ankle.
3. I think I have a cold. My throat is **sore / broken.**
4. The soccer ball hit me in the face. I had a **sprained / bloody** nose.
5. I ran ten miles this morning. Now I have a **hurt / pain** in my knee.
6. A baseball hit Carlos in the face. He has a **bloody / black** eye.
7. After Celia cut her hand, she was in **hurt /pain.**
8. I carried the sofa upstairs. Now my back is **broken / sore.**

❷ Put the conversations in order. Write numbers.

1. _____ Can you bring him in at 3:00?
    _____ OK. What's the problem?
    _____ My brother hurt his back.
    _1_ I'd like to make an appointment.
    _____ Sure. We'll be there at three.

2. _____ The doctor can see her right away.
    _____ My friend was in a car accident. I'd like her to see the doctor.
    _____ She's OK, but she has a black eye and her back hurts.
    _____ Good. We'll be there in ten minutes.
    _____ How is she?

3. _____ Can you come in at 7:00 this evening?
    _____ I'd like to see the doctor.
    _____ What's the matter?
    _____ I'll be there.
    _____ A dog bit me this morning.

4. _____ My ankle hurts. I think I sprained it.
    _____ I need to see the doctor.
    _____ What happened?
    _____ Where does it hurt?
    _____ The doctor can see you at 3:00 this afternoon.
    _____ I slipped and fell in the shower.

③ Complete the sentences. Choose answers from the box.

take an aspirin	drink tea with honey	wait a day or two	go to bed and rest
~~take cold medicine~~	go to the emergency room	see a doctor	

1. A: I have a bad cold.

   B: When I have a cold, I usually _____ *take cold medicine* _____.

2. A: I have a headache.

   B: You should _____.

3. A: Alan has a bad cold. He's really tired all the time.

   B: He should _____.

4. A: I have a sore throat.

   B: When I have a sore throat, I always _____.

5. A: I have headaches every day when I wake up. They get worse all day.

   B: She should _____.

6. A: I think I broke my leg. I can't stand on it.

   B: You should _____. *OR*   You shouldn't

   _____.

④ Answer the questions. Write about yourself. Use complete sentences.

1. When was the last time you were sick?

   _____

2. What was the problem?

   _____

3. What did you do about it?

   _____

4. When was the last time you saw a doctor?

   _____

5. What did the doctor tell you to do?

   _____

6. What do you usually do when you have a headache?

   _____

❶ Complete the sentences. Use _must_ or _must not_.

1. **NO PARKING**

   This sign means you _____ must not park _____ here.

2. **BUCKLE UP!**

   This sign means that you _____ seat belts.

3. **DO NOT ENTER**

   This sign means that you _____ this street.

4. **SPEED LIMIT 65 MPH**

   This sign means that you _____ less than 65 miles per hour.

5. **Employees: Wash hands before leaving restroom**

   This sign means that workers _____ their hands.

6. **NO TALKING**

   This sign means that you _____ here.

❷ Fix the problems in the sentences. If the sentence is correct, write _correct_.

1. You don't have to have a license to drive a car.

   You have to have a license to drive a car. OR _You must have a license to drive a car._

2. You must park in a No Parking area.

   _____

3. You must see a doctor if you have a cold.

   _____

4. You have to go to the emergency room if you break your arm.

   _____

5. We don't have to be on time to class.

   _____

6. You must stop for a green light.

   _____

❸ Bubble the correct answers.

		a	b	c
1. All eight-year-old children in the U.S. _____ attend school.	a) must b) don't have to c) must not	○	○	○
2. Children over 18 years of age _____ attend school.	a) must b) don't have to c) must not	○	○	○
3. Healthy drivers _____ park in a handicapped parking spot.	a) must b) don't have to c) must not	○	○	○
4. If you have a car, you _____ walk to work.	a) must b) don't have to c) must not	○	○	○
5. Parents _____ take care of their children.	a) must b) don't have to c) must not	○	○	○
6. If you want to be rich, you _____ save money.	a) must b) don't have to c) must not	○	○	○
7. Police say we _____ drive faster than the speed limit.	a) must b) don't have to c) must not	○	○	○

❹ Tell the person what to do. Use *must* or *must not*.

1. That coffee's very, very hot. You
   must not drink it.

2. You _____ to music on headphones while driving a forklift.

3. The man is hurt. He _____ to the hospital.

4. The driver _____ right.

5 **For each sign, tell what not to do and why.**

1. A: Wait a minute!

   B: What's the matter?

   A: *Don't park* here.

   B: Why not?

   A: If you park here, you might
   get a ticket .

2. A: Watch out!

   B: What's the matter?

   A: _____ here.

   B: Why not?

   A: If you run here, you might
   _____ .

DO NOT PASS

SPEED LIMIT 30

3. A: Watch out!

   B: What's the matter?

   A: _____ here.

   B: Why not?

   A: If you pass here, you might
   _____ .

4. A: Wait a minute!

   B: What's the problem.

   A: _____ .

   B: Why not?

   A: You might _____ .

DO NOT ENTER

5. A: Stop!

   B: What's the matter.

   A: _____ that street.

   B: Why not?

   A: If you go in there, you might
   _____ .

6. A: Watch out.

   B: What's the problem.

   A: _____ here.

   B: Why not?

   A: If you turn left, you might
   _____ .

Emergencies

1 **Complete the conversations. Use the simple past and past continuous.**

1. A: What happened to you?

   B: _I hurt my elbow_ **while** _playing tennis_ .
   (hurt elbow, play tennis)

2. A: What happened to the man?

   B: _____ while
   _____ .(slip and fall,
   walk to work)

3. A: How did he get hurt?

   B: _____ while
   _____ .(hurt wrist, ride
   his bicycle)

4. A: Why was he late to work?

   B: _____ while
   _____ .(have accident,
   drive to work)

5. A: What's wrong with you?

   B: _____ while
   _____ .(sprain ankle,
   play soccer)

6. A: Why was he so happy?

   B: _____ while
   _____ . (find wallet,
   clean the garage)

❷ Match the words with the correct example or definition.

1. very serious problem __b__
2. pneumonia _____
3. major surgery _____
4. regular checkup _____
5. currently _____
6. lower leg problem _____
7. medication _____
8. arthritis _____
9. medical history _____
10. regularly _____

a. sprained ankle
b. ~~emergency~~
c. aspirin
d. pain in the hands or back
e. a paper completed by a patient
f. hip operation
g. doctor visit once a year
h. every day
i. an illness in the chest area
j. right now

❸ Read the medicine label. Circle *True* or *False*.

Dr. Frank Nappi   Fill date: 03/11/06

BICEROL BR

INGREDIENTS: bicerol acetate

Take three capsules daily with meals.

WARNING: Do not drink alcoholic beverages while taking this medicine.

Store at room temperature.

Discard date: 06/06/07

1. This is an over-the-counter medicine.   True   (False)
2. The patient should take a capsule once a day.   True   False
3. The patient bought the medicine on March 11, 2006.   True   False
4. The patient should throw the medicine away by June 6, 2007.   True   False
5. The patient should take the medicine with water.   True   False
6. The medicine is for Frank Nappi.   True   False
7. The patient can drink alcohol with this medicine.   True   False
8. The medicine should be stored at room temperature.   True   False

Review

❶ Bubble the correct answers.

a   b   c

1. I ran a ten-mile race. Afterwards, my _____ were really sore.
   a) lips   b) hands   c) legs   ○ ○ ○

2. If you _____ on the ice, you might get hurt.
   a) fall   b) will fall   c) were falling   ○ ○ ○

3. Where were you going at 7:00? I _____ to school.
   a) went   b) was going   c) go   ○ ○ ○

4. To get married in New York, you _____ be 18 years old.
   a) should   b) need   c) must   ○ ○ ○

5. If your clothes are clean, you _____ wash them.
   a) don't have to   b) must   c) should   ○ ○ ○

❷ Read the story. Answer the questions. Use complete sentences.

My Emergency Room Visit

When someone mentions an emergency room, I think about the time I hurt my ankle while playing soccer. It had been a difficult game, but we were winning. As I was running down the field, I tripped and fell. I felt a sudden pain in my ankle and heard a crunching sound. Strangely, it didn't hurt that much. But when I tried to walk off of the field, I wasn't able to stand up. A couple of my teammates carried me off the field.

An ambulance took me to the hospital. While we were riding, an EMT took my blood pressure and asked me a lot of questions. At the hospital, a nurse asked me if my head hurt and I laughed. "No, but my leg sure does!" I guess he just wanted to be sure I didn't have a concussion. While we were waiting for the doctor, he helped me fill out the registration forms.

Next, they sent me to the fourth floor for X-rays. When I got back downstairs, the emergency room doctor was waiting for me. He told me that I didn't have a broken ankle. I was really glad! But I had sprained it very badly, and I wouldn't be able to play soccer for a long time. All in all, that emergency room visit lasted over four hours, but I'm fine today, so I can't complain.

1. How did Joe hurt his ankle? *He fell while he was playing soccer.*

2. What did the EMT do? _____ .

3. Did Joe have a concussion? _____ .

4. What happened on the fourth floor? _____ .

5. Did Joe have a sprained ankle? _____ .

6. How long was he in the emergency room? _____ .

Critical Thinking

7. How do you think Joe felt about his emergency room visit?

_____ .

On the Job

Chapter 9

Vocabulary

1 **Complete the sentences.**

1. I'm going to send __g__ .
2. They have to solve _____ .
3. She is trying to open _____ .
4. He didn't catch _____ .
5. I don't like changing _____ .
6. They are painting _____ .
7. Please carry _____ .
8. I have to read _____ .
9. We didn't study for _____ .
10. I filled out _____ .

a. this box for me.
b. the test.
c. an application form.
d. a difficult problem.
e. diapers.
f. any fish.
g. ~~a fax.~~
h. this book for English class.
i. the jar.
j. the living room.

2 **Complete the sentences. Use a verb and a preposition. You will use some prepositions more than once.**

Verbs	Prepositions
look put turn take bring ~~wake~~ drop hand pick run	off back out into in down on up

1. Did you ___wake___ ___up___ early this morning?
2. You can _____ _____ his phone number in the phone book.
3. Will you _____ _____ souvenirs when you visit Mexico?
4. I often _____ _____ friends in the supermarket.
5. Don't forget to _____ _____ your hat. It's cold today.
6. Please _____ _____ this package at the post office for me.
7. The bus will _____ you _____ at the corner.
8. Please _____ _____ the television. I want to go to sleep.
9. How much tax did they _____ _____ of your pay?
10. The test is over. It's time to _____ _____ your papers.

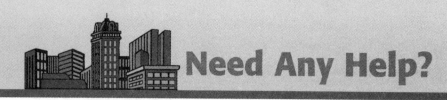

Need Any Help?

① Complete the conversation. Use *will* for offers to help.

1. A: David doesn't know how to fix the TV.

   B: Don't worry. _____*I'll fix it*_____ for him.

2. A: I can't open this jar.

   B: Here. _____ for you.

3. A: I don't know how to change the baby's diaper.

   B: No problem. _____ for you.

4. A: Lisa can't find Jack's name in the phone book.

   B: That's OK. _____ for her.

5. A: I don't know how to send this fax.

   B: Don't worry. _____ for you.

6. A: My father is too old to cut the grass.

   B: No problem. _____ for him.

② Rewrite the sentences using object pronouns after the prepositions.

1. Are you making dinner for Peter and Lisa?

   Are you making dinner for them?

2. Did they talk to the Bakers?

   _____

3. Did they complain about the food?

   _____

4. Was the manager talking to Jack?

   _____

5. Do you live near the park?

   _____

6. Please send this fax to Mary.

   _____

7. I'm going to sit next to Frank.

   _____

3 Put the conversations in order. Write numbers.

1. _____ Then you paint each wall from the left side to the right side.

_____ Next, you mix the paint completely.

_____ Sure, I'd be happy to. First, you put a cloth on the floor.

_____ OK. I mixed the paint. Now what?

_1_ I never painted a room before. Can you help me?

2. _____ OK. Then you take off the old diaper and clean the baby up.

_____ I think the floor is safer.

_____ How do you change a diaper?

_____ Right. Then what?

_____ Just put on the clean diaper.

_____ It's not hard. First, you put the new diaper and a clean cloth on the changing table or on the floor.

3. _____ Last name first, right?

_____ No. The manager will do that for you.

_____ Could you show me how to fill out this time card?

_____ OK. Do I have to add up the hours at the bottom?

_____ Sure. First, fill in your name at the top.

_____ That's right. Then write in the number of hours you worked each day.

4. _____ OK. My feet are apart.

_____ Like this?

_____ Next, you hold the bat behind your right shoulder.

_____ Could you show me how to hit a baseball?

_____ It's not easy, but I'll try. First, you stand with your feet wide apart.

_____ That's right. Now remember to keep your eye on the ball. Don't look away.

4 Circle the correct words.

1. Jack is talking, but no one is listening. He is talking to **themselves / (himself.)**

2. Linda doesn't need any help with the homework. She can do it by **herself / itself.**

3. You don't have to close the door. The door will close by **itself / yourself.**

4. My aunt and uncle don't have any children at home. They live by **themselves / itself.**

5. No one cooks for me. I cook for **myself / themselves.**

5 Bubble the correct answers.

	a	b

1. Q: Is _____ home?

   a) anybody   b) someone   ○ ○

   A: No, _____ is home.

   a) someone   b) no one   ○ ○

2. Q: Is _____ watching TV?

   a) no one   b) anyone   ○ ○

   A: Yes, _____ is.

   a) somebody   b) anyone   ○ ○

3. Q: Did _____ study for the test?

   a) anyone   b) nobody   ○ ○

   A: No, _____ did.

   a) no one   b) someone   ○ ○

4. Q: Is _____ sitting in this seat?

   a) anyone   b) nobody   ○ ○

   A: Yes, _____ is.

   a) everyone   b) someone   ○ ○

5. Q: Did _____ go home early?

   a) no one   b) anyone   ○ ○

   A: Yes, _____ went home early.

   a) anyone   b) everyone   ○ ○

6. Q: Is _____ at lunch now?

   a) nobody   b) anyone   ○ ○

   A: No, _____ is still in the office.

   a) anyone   b) everyone   ○ ○

7. Q: Is _____ waiting for the bus?

   a) anybody   b) no one   ○ ○

   A: Yes, _____ is waiting.

   a) anyone   b) someone   ○ ○

8. Q: Is _____ absent today?

   a) anyone   b) nobody   ○ ○

   A: Yes, _____ is.

   a) someone   b) anyone   ○ ○

9. Q: Is _____ tired?

   a) nobody   b) anybody   ○ ○

   A: No, _____ is tired.

   a) someone   b) no one   ○ ○

10. Q: Is _____ using the fax machine?

   a) no one   b) anyone   ○ ○

   A: Yes, _____ is using it right now.

   a) someone   b) everyone   ○ ○

6 Complete the conversation. Explain how to make or do something. Use your own experience.

A: I don't know how to _____.

B: No problem. I'll show you how. First, you _____.

A: OK. _____

B: Next, you _____.

A: _____

B: Then you _____.

A: Thanks!

1 **Complete the sentences with the correct possessive adjectives and possessive pronouns.**

1. Lisa has a dog. That's ___her___ dog over there. It's ___hers___ .

2. You can keep this pen. It's _____ pen now. It's _____ .

3. Give me my parents' keys. Give me _____ keys. Give me _____ .

4. I like Dick's new car. I love _____ car. I want one just like _____ .

5. There's a new computer on my desk. It's _____ computer. It's _____ .

6. You and I have the same birthday. It's _____ birthday. It's _____ .

2 **Complete the conversations with the correct object pronouns and possessive pronouns.**

1. A: Take this book to Jim. It's ___his___ (he).
   B: OK. I'll take it to ___him___ (he) right now.

2. A: Can I use _____ (you) laptop for a few minutes?
   B: Sure. I'll bring it to _____ (you) right away.

3. A: Please give this address book to your father. It's _____ (he).
   B: OK. I'll give it to _____ (he) tonight.

4. A: Please hand me that file. It's _____ (I) and I need it.
   B: OK. Here's _____ (you) file.

5. A: Take this letter to Rob. It's _____ (he) letter.
   B: I'll take it to _____ (he) later.

6. A: Could you give these cookies to the children? They're _____ (they).
   B: Sure. I'll give the cookies to _____ (they) in a minute.

3 Fix the mistakes in the incorrect sentences. If the sentence is correct, write *correct*.

1. A: I read your evaluation form.

   You works very slowly.

   B: I'm sorry.

   I try to work faster.

   A: Please try.

   It's important

   B: I promise to try.

   I do my best.

   A: *Correct*

   You work very slowly.

   B: _____

   _____

   A: _____

   _____

   B: _____

   _____

2. A: Will I talk with you about something?.

   You make a lot of mistakes.

   B: I'm sorry.

   I know it will be a problem.

   I'll be more careful.

   I try to do better work.

   A: I talk to you about it again next week.

   Please come to my office on Tuesday.

   B: Thanks, I do that.

   A: _____

   _____

   B: _____

   _____

   _____

   _____

   A: _____

   _____

   B: _____

4 Write sentences. Use *will* to make promises.

1. A: I notice you're often late to work.

   B: _____

2. A: Don't stay out too late tonight.

   B: _____

3. A: Your handwriting is hard to read.

   B: _____

4. A: You have had two car accidents in a year.

   B: _____

The Office

❶ Complete the sentences with *so* or *because*.

1. I was tired _____ I worked so hard all day.

2. I didn't have any money _____ I got a job.

3. John wanted some new clothes _____ he went shopping.

4. Celia can't come to class _____ she is sick.

5. The company closed _____ a lot of people lost their jobs.

6. We stayed home last night _____ there was a good show on TV.

7. I woke up early _____ I had to go to work.

8. I don't like ice cream _____ I never eat it.

9. Frank is a doctor _____ he goes to the hospital every day.

10. He became a doctor _____ he likes to take care of people.

❷ Read the conversations. Complete the messages.

1. A: Hepworth Hospital. Alice speaking.

   B: This is Tony Calarco. I'm calling for my wife, Marie. She can't come to work today.

   A: Oh, I'm sorry. What's wrong?

   B: She has the flu. Please tell her manager, Ms. Martin.

   A: OK, I'll tell her.

   Message
   To: _____Ms. Martin_____
   From: _____
   Message: _____
   _____
   _____
   Urgent _____

2. A: This is Kent speaking.

   B: Hi, Kent. This is Lisa. I need to talk to Mr. Blake right away.

   A: OK. I'll give him the message.

   B: Please do it as soon as you can. It's urgent.

   A: Will do.

   Message
   From: _____
   Message: _____
   _____
   _____
   Urgent _____

3 Circle the correct words.

1. Please remember to **turn /** (**turn off**) the lights.

2. You should **look / look up** that word in the dictionary.

3. Be careful. Don't **drop / drop off** that glass.

4. Alice **took / took off** her umbrella because it looked like rain.

5. Please **turn / turn on** left at the corner.

6. Who did you **run / run into** at the mall?

7. Would you **drop / drop off** these boxes at the post office?

8. **Look / Look up** at that beautiful carpet!

9. Roger can **run / run into** ten miles without stopping.

10. I **took / took off** my coat because it was very warm in the room.

4 Complete the sentences. Use words from the box.

junk	snail	sales	assistant	joking	opportunity
take-home	urgent	gross	~~withhold~~	message	

1. I wish they wouldn't _____ withhold _____ so much money from my paycheck.

2. This is very important. In fact, it's _____ .

3. A salesperson wanted to talk to me about a business _____ .

4. I work as an office _____ .

5. E-mail is a lot faster than _____ mail.

6. I'd like to leave a _____ for Ms. Martin.

7. Your _____ pay is always a lot larger than your _____ pay.

8. You're not serious. You're _____ .

9. I work in a _____ office.

10. I always recycle my _____ mail.

1 Bubble the correct answers.

a　b　c

1. This is my pen. That one over there is _____ .
   a) you 　　　　b) your 　　　　c) yours
   ○　○　○

2. Please bring your dictionaries _____ when you're finished with them.
   a) about 　　　　b) back 　　　　c) up
   ○　○　○

3. Give them this map. _____ need it.
   a) They 　　　　b) Their 　　　　c) Theirs
   ○　○　○

4. Is _____ home right now?
   a) nobody 　　　　b) no one 　　　　c) anyone
   ○　○　○

5. She hurt _____ when she tripped on a rock.
   a) himself 　　　　b) itself 　　　　c) herself
   ○　○　○

2 Read the story. Then circle the correct answers.

The Life of a Manager

Eileen Carter is a manager in a large department store. She likes her job a lot, but sometimes she remembers how nice it was not being the boss. She has to come to work early every day to prepare work schedules and read her e-mail. She also has reports to write and employee evaluations to complete. Sometimes employees can't come to work because they are sick or because of a family emergency. Then she has to do their jobs as well as her own.

But all in all, Ms. Carter is happy with her position. Her salary is higher than it was two years ago. Her boss tells her she is doing a good job. The most difficult part of the job for her is the employee evaluations. She has no problem talking to people about attendance and punctuality, but she doesn't like talking about appearance. It feels too personal to her. Ms. Carter heard that her boss may be leaving. She is thinking about applying for the job.

1. Ms. Carter works for a large **supermarket / department store.**
2. Ms. Carter goes to work early in order to **read her e-mail / talk to her boss.**
3. When an employee is sick, she **calls their home / does their job.**
4. She doesn't like to talk to employees about their **appearance / attendance.**
5. Ms. Carter may **fire one of her employees / take a new job.**

Critical Thinking
6. Would you like a job like Ms. Carter's? Why or why not? _____

Vocabulary

1 Complete the lists with words from the box. Use each word once.

~~punctual~~	outgoing	sew	aide	smile	clerk	handshake
~~eye contact~~	organized	assistant	play the guitar	~~salesperson~~		
dependable	~~type~~	posture	fix things			

1. Nonverbal communication

   eye contact

   _____

   _____

   _____

2. Personal strengths

   punctual

   _____

   _____

   _____

3. Skills and abilities

   type

   _____

   _____

   _____

4. Jobs

   salesperson

   _____

   _____

   _____

2 Complete the conversation. Use words from the box.

benefits	salary	working conditions	~~interview~~	résumé
hire	applicant	weaknesses	application	strengths

A: What happened after you got to the _____interview_____ ?

B: First, I filled out the _____ . Then the interviewer asked about my _____ and _____ .

A: Did she say how much you'd make?

B: We didn't discuss _____ , but she said health care and other _____ are paid by the company.

A: Well, that's good. What are the _____ like?

B: The office is clean and attractive and everyone seems very friendly.

A: What did she think of your _____ ?

B: After she read it, she said she'd like to _____ me.

A: That's great!

B: But I'm not the only _____ . I might not get the job.

Skills and Abilities

❶ Fix the mistakes in the incorrect sentences. If the sentence is correct, write *correct*.

1. We were able to relax after we finish our last exam tomorrow.

   We will be able to relax after we finish our last exam tomorrow.

2. Ellen can swim when she was five years old.

   _____

3. My parents was able to learn English very quickly.

   _____

4. Roberto can sleep late last semester because he didn't have any morning classes.

   _____

5. Celia can cook better than her sister.

   _____

6. You were able to speak fluently a year or two from now.

   _____

7. My sister was able to save enough money to go to Paris last year.

   _____

8. I practiced a lot last year and now I was able to win every game of tennis I play.

   _____

9. When he lived in Mexico, Carlos can speak Spanish all the time.

   _____

10. When you finish this class, you will can take the next class.

   _____

❷ Match the words with the same meaning.

1. __h__ a must
2. _____ repair
3. _____ preferred
4. _____ position
5. _____ aide

6. _____ title
7. _____ fluent
8. _____ skill
9. _____ minimum
10. _____ classified

a. helper
b. clear and quick
c. least
d. fix
e. help wanted

f. a plus
g. name
h. ~~necessary~~
i. opening
j. ability

③ Answer the questions about the ads. Use complete sentences.

WANTED: *Experienced Cook*

Must be organized, energetic.
2 years experience req.   English speaker pref.
Experience with Italian and Chinese cooking necessary.
Must be able to handle 100 orders an hour.
Tues - Sat, 12 P.M. to 8 P.M.   Position begins immediately.
Call (707) 555-9763

---

1. What skills are required for the job?

    The person must know how to cook Italian and Chinese food.

2. How much experience does the job require?

    _____

3. What kind of person are they looking for?

    _____

4. What must the person be able to do?

    _____

5. Is the position full-time or part-time?

    _____

WANTED: *Taxi Driver*

Must be able to work nights.
Clean driving record req.   1 year experience pref.
Taxi Drivers License necessary.
Experience repairing cars a plus.
Own cell phone needed.
M – F, 12 A.M. to 8 A.M.
Call (505) 555-4339

---

6. What kind of license must the person have?

    _____

7. How much experience would they like?

    _____

8. What other skill would they like?

    _____

9. What other requirements are there?

    _____

10. Is the position full-time or part-time?

    _____

Job Application Form

1 **Read the conversation and complete the application on page 86.**

Rita: Hey, Andy. Could you help me out?

Andy: Sure. What's up?

Rita: I have a job interview this afternoon. Would you mind helping me practice for it?

Andy: Not at all. What can I do?

Rita: Just look at my application and ask me questions about it so I can practice talking about myself.

Andy: Sure. What is your full name?

Rita: Rita J. Peterson.

Andy: And where do you live?

Rita: At 79 Main Street in Foxboro, Massachusetts.

Andy: And what's the zip there?

Rita: 02250.

Andy: And how long have you lived there?

Rita: Since 2004.

Andy: And your phone number?

Rita: It's 666-907-7758.

Andy: Tell me about your education.

Rita: I have finished one year at Foxboro Business Academy in Foxboro, Massachusetts. I attended from 1999 to 2000. I don't have a degree yet.

Andy: Have you ever had a job?

Rita: Yes, I've had two jobs. My latest job was as a teacher's aide from 2002 to 2003 at Helping Little Hands at 1500 Canton Street in Boston. My supervisor was Bruce Davidson. His number is 666-910-6388. My job was taking care of young children.

Andy: And what was your first job?

Rita: From 2001 to 2002 I was a clerk at Gracy's Department Store on Massachusetts Avenue in Boston. My boss was Alice Armonk at 666-910-8472. I sold sweaters in the women's clothing department.

Andy: And when are you available to work?

Rita: I'd like to work part-time, evenings and weekends.

Andy: Thank you Ms. Peterson.

Rita: Hey, thanks a lot, Andy!

APPLICATION FOR EMPLOYMENT

Personal Information

NAME: _____ _____ _____
Last · First · Middle Initial

STREET ADDRESS: _____ CITY: _____ STATE: _____

ZIP: _____ HOW LONG HAVE YOU LIVED AT THIS ADDRESS? _____ TEL. NO.: _____

Education

LAST SCHOOL ATTENDED: _____ LOCATION: _____

DATES: _____ LAST GRADE COMPLETED: _____ GRADUATED: _____

Work History

EMPLOYER: _____ LOCATION: _____ TEL. NO.: _____

SUPERVISOR: _____ DATES WORKED: _____ JOB TITLE: _____

DUTIES: _____

Work History

EMPLOYER: _____ LOCATION: _____ TEL. NO.: _____

SUPERVISOR: _____ DATES WORKED: _____ JOB TITLE: _____

DUTIES: _____

Availability

FULL-TIME: [   ]   PART-TIME: [   ]   WEEKENDS: [   ]   EVENINGS: [   ]

❷ Circle the correct words.

1. A teller **sells food /** (**makes change.**)
2. A taxi driver **picks up passengers / delivers goods.**
3. A deli clerk **takes inventory / makes sandwiches.**
4. A teacher's aide **must drive a car / must be patient.**
5. A receptionist **greets visitors / takes inventory.**
6. A cook **answers phones / plans menus.**
7. A lawyer **writes contracts / must speak two languages.**
8. A sales clerk **takes inventory / takes messages.**
9. A parking attendant **collects parking fees / sells cars.**
10. An auto mechanic **repairs brakes / writes checks.**

❸ Put the conversations in order. Write numbers.

1. _____ What did you do on that job?
   _1_ What was your last job?
   _____ I was a counter person.
   _____ What were you doing before that?
   _____ I was attending school.
   _____ I sold coffee and bakery goods.

2. _____ What did you sell?
   _____ What did you do before that?
   _____ What was your last job?
   _____ Before that, I worked in a factory.
   _____ I was a salesperson.
   _____ I sold cars and trucks.

3. _____ I made Italian food.
   _____ Before that, I was a deli clerk.
   _____ What kind of food did you cook?
   _____ What was your last job?
   _____ What were you doing before that?
   _____ I was a cook.

4. _____ And what did you do before that?
   _____ I took food orders and brought people food.
   _____ And what did you do on that job?
   _____ What was your last job?
   _____ Before that, I worked in my mother's bakery.
   _____ I was a waitress.

❹ Bubble the correct answer.

                                                           a   b

1. We _____ when the dog woke us up.
   a) slept   b) were sleeping   ◯   ◯

2. I _____ in while the teacher was explaining the lesson.
   a) walked   b) was walking   ◯   ◯

3. The wind _____ hard when the tree fell over.
   a) blew   b) was blowing   ◯   ◯

4. The rain _____ while we were walking home.
   a) was starting   b) started   ◯   ◯

5. Ron _____ soccer when he suddenly got a bad headache.
   a) was playing   b) played   ◯   ◯

6. Bill was reading when Lisa _____ the light.
   a) was turning off   b) turned off   ◯   ◯

The Job Interview

1 **Write *B* in front of each *benefit* and *W* in front of each *working condition*.**

1. __B__ health insurance
2. _____ a holiday bonus
3. _____ a 9-to-5 schedule
4. _____ a retirement plan
5. _____ a nice boss
6. _____ paid vacation
7. _____ hourly pay
8. _____ a clean safe workplace
9. _____ paid holidays
10. _____ interesting coworkers

2 **Match the words with the same meaning.**

1. __g__ organized
2. _____ truthful
3. _____ dependable
4. _____ bright
5. _____ friendly
6. _____ punctual
7. _____ shy
8. _____ in charge of
9. _____ polite
10. _____ creative

a. reliable
b. always on time
c. quiet
d. nice
e. full of new ideas
f. honest
g. ~~carefully prepared~~
h. fast learner
i. responsible for
j. outgoing

❸ Circle the correct word(s).

PERSONNEL DIRECTOR

A: Tell me a little about yourself.

B: You mean about my **skills** / **schedule** and experience?

A: No. I can see that on the **advertisement** / **application form.** Tell me about your **position** / **personality.** What are your personal **benefits** / **strengths**?

B: Well, **I'm very bright / I have a driver's license.**

A: That's good. I'm happy to her that. What else?

B: I am **30 years old / very organized.**

A: I see. And what **benefits** / **location** are you interested in?

B: I have two children, so **grooming** / **health insurance** is important to me.

A: What was your **salary** / **schedule** on your last job?

B: I worked 12 P.M. to 8 P.M. five days a week.

A: And did you work any **overtime** / **retirement** hours?

B: Yes, but only on weekends.

A: Thanks for coming in. We'll call you in a day or two.

B: Thank you very much.

❹ Describe some working conditions and benefits you would like in your next job. Give a reason for each choice.

1. First working condition: _____

   Reason: _____

2. Second working condition: _____

   Reason: _____

3. First benefit: _____

   Reason: _____

4. Second benefit: _____

   Reason: _____

Review

1 Bubble the correct answers.

		a b c

1. Do you pay extra for _____ ?
   a) interviews   b) benefits   c) overtime hours   ○ ○ ○
2. Please _____ me next Monday.
   a) file   b) contact   c) speak   ○ ○ ○
3. I am _____ and always do a good job.
   a) reliable   b) shy   c) not responsible   ○ ○ ○
4. I _____ type 40 words a minute.
   a) can   b) know to   c) able to   ○ ○ ○
5. While I was working at Claire's, I _____ how to take inventory.
   a) will be able to learn   b) could learn   c) learned   ○ ○ ○

2 Read the story. Answer the questions. Use complete sentences.

Carla's Next Job

Carla likes her present job, but she is always thinking ahead. Careful planning will mean that she can move to a better job. Anything she does to prepare herself for a new job will help her in her present position. For example, if she takes a computer course, she will be able to do a better job at work. If she improves her language skills, her employers will know she is interested in advancing in the company.

Carla also reads the classified section of the newspaper every week. There she finds listings of job openings that might be good for her. She notices how much they're paying and what benefits they're offering. Then, if her yearly evaluation is very good, she might ask for a raise or an increase in benefits similar to the ones she has read about in the newspaper.

When she decides to leave her present job, she will tell her employer at least two weeks ahead of time. This will give the company time to hire someone to replace her. She may need a recommendation, and it's a good idea to remain on friendly terms.

1. Does Carla like the job she has now? _Yes, she does._____

2. How can preparing for a new job help her now? _____

3. Why should Carla improve her language skills? _____

4. What does she learn from the classified ads? _____

5. What can Carla do with this information? _____

6. What should she do when she leaves her present job? _____

Critical Thinking

7. How do you like your present job? What could you do to make it better for yourself? _____